'You can certainly count on one sale, I can promise you that' —
New York Times best-selling author Bill Bryson

Also by Jon Breakfield

Naked Europe:
In the Hunt for the *Real* Europe and Romance

KEY WEST:

Tequila, a Pinch of Salt and a Quirky Slice of America

by

Jon Breakfield

KW
Press

To Mike and Alicyn, who loved Key West.
John V M Rubin for his support all these years.
And Ian and *Sally!*

ACKNOWLEDGEMENTS

The following people deserve a special mention: Popcorn Joe (without him there would be no book), Alberto and Joan (without them there would be no Villa Alberto), B.O. for rescuing us on the high seas, and O.J. Dave for his education on all things IT.

I would also like to shout a big 'GIVE IT UP!' to everyone who was on the pier back then (and many still are): Don and Shirley Sullivan, Will Soto, O.J. Dave, Deidre & Peter, Gus & Jeanne, Claudia Richards, Buschi, Annabel, Janine, Dominique, Duffy, Joanne Albert, Clara Taylor, Larry Batts, Harry Powell, Carollee, Charles Byarlay, Ray, Love 22, The Cookie Lady, Ibashi-I, Dan the deaf magician, Whistling Tom, Suzanne Buxton, Ginger & Louie, Noodleman Ron, Javier, Annie Summers, Helena Petersen, Michel Delgado, Joanne Hasman, Monica, Tim Eric, Ben Benton, Anna (violin), Dale Pritchard, Dennis the Bagpiper, The White Statue Man, Angela, Beth, Joyce Straiton, Harriet and Robert, and rest in peace: Tony, Garnett and Len.

CHAPTER 1

The wind is deafening now. Howling. Screeching. This is Hades on earth and we are both terrified of the unknown. How long can this go on?

We peek out the crack in our boarded-up front window. The tree across the lane is bent sideways and coconuts shoot by like cannonballs. Why hadn't we evacuated when we first heard the hurricane was coming our way?

The wailing grows and grows and grows. Louder than before. Different than before. A baneful roar that is threatening to blow our house away. Then we hear a horrific splitting sound and there's a tremendous crash on our tin roof.

And our front door explodes open.

We rush the door and attempt to force it closed, but the hurricane fights back with unnatural strength. This monster is so relentless we have to lie flat on our backs and use our legs to wedge the door shut. As we're down there, frightened out of our minds and soaked to the skin, my life flashes in front of me. Curiously, it screeches to a halt at the part that got us into this mess in the first place.

* * *

'We don't care where it is,' I said, glancing over at my wife, Gabrielle, 'as long as it's south. Anywhere south.'

The young lass working the desk at Barrhead Travel, in Glasgow, giggled, squirmed in her seat, then tugged on the front of a blouse that was at least two sizes too small. Her name was Bridget, and she presented a sunny disposition on a crap-weather day.

'You'll be wanting the sun, then?' she said.

I glanced over at our brolly leaking all over the carpet. It was the first week of January. It had been pissing off and on for months -- since right near the end of the hosepipe ban.

'Sun is indeed what we're after,' I said. 'Shorts, tropical drinks with little umbrellas sticking out the top. That sort of thing. We'd kill for a really bad sunburn right about now.'

Bridget hooked her hair behind her ear, shifted a copy of *heat* out of the way and attacked the computer keyboard.

After banging away on the keys long enough to programme the space shuttle, Bridget turned to us: 'How 'bout Ibiza?'

Gabrielle gave me a terrified look.

'I fear we're too old for Ibiza.'

Bridget assaulted the keyboard again and presented us with winter-sun destination number two: 'Benidorm?'

'Too young for Benidorm in the winter.'

'How 'bout Playa de las Américas?'

'Do either of us look like we're between 18 and 30?' I asked.

'Your wife does. You definitely don't,' Bridget said candidly.

Gabrielle laughed.

'Magaluf?'

'Thanks, but no thanks.'

'Playa del Inglés?'

I shook my head.

Bridget crinkled her nose at me: 'Thought you said it didn't matter as long as it was south?'

'Did. Sorry.'

Bridget consulted her computer again, then her eyes lit up: 'Got just the place for you,' she squealed. 'You want sun. I've found you sun. You, Mr and Mrs Breakfield, are going to Key West, Florida. It's a tiny island at the end of the Florida Keys. I can get you a great fare, but you'll have to find your own accommodation.'

'Key West! Don't they get hurricanes there?'

'Hurricanes?' Bridget laughed. 'It's winter. Hurricane season doesn't start till June. Plus, they never hit Key West.'

Then Bridget became serious: 'But I should warn you about something. Key West may have an American flag stuck in the middle of it, but it's nothing like America.'

* * *

Less than a week later, Gabrielle and I were sitting on an old cement dock in Key West, basking in late-afternoon wall-to-wall sun, our bare feet dangling down towards the Tanqueray-clear waters of the Gulf of Mexico. No stress. No cares. No umbrellas.

I had a beer in my hand that I had smuggled out of a nearby pub. Gabrielle had a margarita -- same modus operandi.

'Key West has serious wow factor,' I said.

'Can't believe we're really here,' Gabrielle said, smiling the world's widest smile.

A light breeze wafted out of Cuba. We could smell the salt in the air. It was 80 degrees Fahrenheit. And the palm trees were doing the Lambada.

I quaffed my beer with great reverence. Gabrielle licked the salt on the rim of her margarita with deep sincerity. We watched as two local kids, brown as berries, fished off the dock for amber jack and mullet. The boys were about ten-years-old and they spoke in Spanish and laughed a lot. When it became too hot for the lads, they simply jumped into the sea and then climbed back up an old tire that was hanging over the side and used as a fender for docking shrimp boats.

What a great place to be a kid.

I pulled out our little guidebook. A colour map informed us that the entrance to the Key West Channel was just to our left, beyond that the coral reef and beyond that, only 90 miles from Key West, Havana, Cuba. As we sat there, letting the tropical air play in our hair and the sun warm our faces, the feeling was one of being at the end of the world. Last stop. End of the line. And nobody even knew we were here (except Bridget, of course).

And we couldn't imagine wanting to be anywhere else on earth.

HONNNK! HONNNK! HONNNK! An air horn sounded and Gabrielle shouted: 'Look!' Off to our right we spotted an impressive yacht as it rounded the corner and slipped out of the harbour at the neighbouring Ocean Key Resort. This was the glass-bottom boat and it was setting off on its daily sunset cruise. A boatload of delirious, pallatic passengers waved wildly at us as the boat motored by. We waved back and toasted them with our drinks. And they all toasted back.

Sailboats cleaved the sparkling waters in front of us, a Coast Guard cutter came down the channel from our left and a vintage biplane pierced the airspace from the direction of the Key West airport and started doing loopty-loops.

We heard a curious plink-plonk sound and turned to see a bloke with dreadlocks playing a steel drum. Mallory Dock and the neighbouring area known as Mallory Square was metamorphosing as various artists, street entertainers and musicians began arriving in rusted out vans, aging pickups and on funky bicycles.

What was this all about?

We dove back into the guide book and discovered that in Key West, every day of the year, an hour or so before sunset, Mallory Square becomes a venue for the 'Sunset Celebration': world-class street theatre, the sale of local arts and crafts, and the worshipping of the doggedly marketed Key West sunset. Were we ever looking forward to this!

Within an hour, the two little local boys had disappeared and beer-swilling grockles had taken their place. The less inebriated formed scrums around the engaging street performers. The pickled milled gooselike among the various craft vendors. And the hard-core drinkers sat in comatose bliss, staring out at the horizon, with now their feet dangling over the edge of the dock.

* * *

Gabrielle and I were watching a sailboat tack lazily in the direction of the setting sun, when suddenly she turned to me.

'Let's not go back.'

'The hotel? No, we'll go have a whole lot of drinks first.'

'No, I mean to Glasgow. Let's not go back. Let's stay here.'

Gabrielle has a wicked sense of humour and I laughed.

'I'm not joking,' she said.

I looked deep into my wife's eyes and they danced with adventure. This had been one of her qualities that had caught my eye when we'd first met. One of the reasons I had married her. She was exhilaratingly spontaneous and not at all afraid of a little adventure.

'Is it the margarita?' I said.

'No. I'm serious. Let's not go back.'

'What about all our stuff?'

'Stuff it!'

'What about your job at the hotel?' I asked.

'They'll replace me with someone from France -- or Poland.'

Gabrielle sipped her margarita, then turned to me with curious subtext. 'What about your job at the airport? Do you like it?'

'Right, I leave in the dark and come home in the dark, and I stand there all day long talking to people flying off to exotic locales.'

We turned our attention to an elderly Cuban fishing off the dock. The old man reeled in his line, checked his bait, then cast it back out into the aquamarine waters. He watched his line for a few moments with great interest, then sat down on an overturned bucket, opened up his bait box and extracted a cool Corona beer.

'Okay,' I said. 'Let's not go back. But what are we going to do for jobs?'

'What does it matter? We'll find something. You only live once.'

'What about a car?'

'You obviously don't need a car in Key West. We'll buy bicycles.'

'What about clothes? We didn't bring much with us.'

'It's a tropical island. How much do you need hanging in the armoire?'

'What about all our crap back in the UK?'

'Bribe family. There will be hell to pay until they realise they have a free place to stay in the Florida Keys.'

This was all starting to sound pretty good, but then I thought of a problem -- a big problem.

'But you don't have a Green Card. You'll be illegal.'

'I know,' Gabrielle said, her eyes twinkling mischievously. 'I bet there's hundreds of people working here illegally.'

And what Gabrielle said right there in many ways summed up an aspect of Key West's spirit. It's a place where anything and everything goes -- plus some. And it's a far-flung island filled with hordes of foreigners and foreign intrigue. The perfect place to live if you are, say, illegal.

I grabbed Gabrielle's hand and we dove into the circus atmosphere that is Mallory Square at sunset. And with a frisson of excitement crackling between us (at least until the next day when we came to our senses) we strolled around this thrillingly colourful part of the world. And we couldn't believe what we saw: jugglers, fire eaters, a tightrope walker, musicians, a cat show, a dog show, a pig show, a bird show, a sword swallower, a guy whistling Amazing Grace, a gargoyle of a man galumphing about balancing a shopping trolley on his face and Statue Man. We also spotted troubadours, minstrels, a young demoiselle playing a violin and a gaggle of arts and crafts folk. There was even a fellow -- of questionable mental health -- weaving baskets, hats and lampshades (same size, same shape) out of palm fronds who went ballistic when an admiring soul innocently tried to snap his photo. And there were palm readers, Tarot card readers and psychics who professed universal peace and tranquillity -- when they weren't at each other's throats for poaching business.

We purchased the world's best orange juice from a guy by the name of O.J. Dave and fought our way through the sweaty bodies and down the dock in the direction of the Key West Aquarium where a little footbridge connects Mallory Square and the neighbouring Hilton Resort and came upon a group of tourists huddled at the edge of the pier. Everyone was staring down into the shallows. Holding sway was a deeply tanned, bare-chested entrepreneurial lowlife. This bloke was none other than 'Fish-Man' and he was the equivalent of the fringe festival, an illegal performer who worked in the wings of the other entertainment by pointing out the brightly coloured tropical fish cruising in and out of the pier. Simply said, he was a remora feeding off the nearby touristic frenzy.

We watched as Fish-Man threw his high-tech chum, which looked curiously like freshly buttered popcorn, down into the water to a flurry of darting creatures and then as they intercepted the fluffy white kernels, he rattled off his trophies: 'There's a Slippery Dick!' All the women gasped as he pointed to a small tropical fish with a blue and yellow stripe that he obviously loved to open his act with. 'And see that one there? That's a barracuda. And over there? Here comes a baby hammerhead! Begs the question "Where's mama?"' Everyone laughed.

Fish-Man pointed out a few more rubbery creatures, then suddenly wheeled on us, smiled an I've-been-sniffing-too-much glue smile and, as we all took a step back, held up an empty Pepsi cup for tips.

When no one would dare venture near him, he shrieked at us: 'Goddamn fucking tourons! Why don't y'all go back up North!'

(We would later learn in Key West parlance a touron is a tourist/moron.)

Fish-Man drove home his sentiments with this colloquial barrage: 'Any you sumbitches snag one of my pets, your corn-fed asses'll be grass and I'll be the lawn mower!'

It goes without saying (although say it I must), the crowd scarpered, scattering a flurry of peckish feral cats who had been peeping at the proceedings from the fragrant safety of a nearby jasmine bush.

As an experiment in subhuman behaviour, I inched a few baby steps towards the now fish-eyed Fish-Man and held out a lonely dollar in my outstretched hand.

'Thank you, sir. Mighty kind of you, sir,' Fish-Man said, snatching the buck with the charm of a moray eel. 'Man's got to make an honest living. Got a narrow window for biz. When there's no sunset, I make no money.' Then, he shot me a searching fish-eyed look: 'Enjoy your stay. Just as soon have you here as some other asshole.'

'I'll take that as a compliment,' I said.

Suddenly a bagpipe wailed in the background, someone blew a conch shell and we all fell silent (Fish-Man put his hand over his heart) and watched, transfixed, as the sun squatted on the horizon and then melted over the backside of the earth.

It was a magical moment.

Everyone spontaneously applauded.

And I kissed Gabrielle.

What an exotic and undeniably unusual place Key West was.

Within a few minutes, as if higher powers were adjusting a dimmer switch up in the heavens, the sky began to slowly smear with ribbons of deep crimsons and rich magentas and lusty shades of cyan. In the distance, way out at sea, a towering thunderhead spit out shards of lightning and a low rumbling rolled our away. The gods were bowling (or moving furniture).

Then a loud scream. Now what! We swivelled around. A fight had broken out between the escape artist and one of the palm readers. The escape artist, in his lack-of-oxygen dotage, had apparently staggered on to the sacrosanct turf occupied by one of the palm readers, a crustacean of a woman with a comparable personality.

'She's going all postal again,' came a friendly, amused voice from behind us.

We turned to see a cheery Elvis Costello look-alike pushing a mobile popcorn cart. His name was Popcorn Joe. A sign on Popcorn Joe's cart read: 'Pretty Good Popcorn'.

Popcorn Joe gave us a welcoming smile. 'Just another day in paradise.'

About now, a multi-generational family from the UK hurried up to purchase popcorn.

We watched Popcorn Joe in action. This was a man who knew his trade. And he really put on a show. As fresh popcorn spit out of the hopper, Joe flapped a white paper bag in the air, swirled a snowdrift-sized amount of popcorn around with an enormous stainless steel popcorn scoop, then excavated a prodigious amount into the maw of the bag: 'That'll be three dollars, please,' Popcorn Joe said, with a *Magnum, P.I.* fluttering of the eyebrows. 'Refills and advice are free.'

Three generations of family stood frozen in place, sunburnt faces aghast, mouths open like baby birds, regarding Popcorn Joe as if he were from the moon (or possibly deeper in the universe), then they smiled politely, paid for their popcorn and scurried off in the direction of the pig show.

Gabrielle motioned with her head towards the scampering family and whispered: 'Grandfather's a Weegie, son-in-law a Geordie.'

'Must be lively around the house on Saturday afternoons.'

A phone rang somewhere. Popcorn Joe rooted through his money pouch and extracted a cell phone the size of a sea cucumber.

'Whaddaya need? How much? Tonight? Yeah, I think I can swing that.'

'What was that all about?' I whispered to Gabrielle. 'Sound as fishy to you as it did to me?'

'Didn't sound much like popcorn business.'

Gabrielle and I took one more peek at the flaming sky, and the crabby palm reader who was trying to throw the chained-up escape artist into the Gulf of Mexico, then turned and hightailed it the hell out of there. We didn't want to still be around after dark.

Laughing, we fled Mallory Square by cutting in between the Waterfront Playhouse and El Meson de Pepe, a tropical outdoor bar/restaurant, where a Latin band was knocking out some *caliente* salsa and locals were throwing back shots of Cuervo. Then we turned left on a bricked alley -- called Wall Street -- and spilled out on to Duval Street.

We had read that Duval Street is the high street of Key West and it stretches from the Gulf of Mexico side of the island to the Atlantic Ocean side of the island, about one mile or so, and it is the spinal cord (and sexual organs) of the Old Town. When you peregrinate and drink on Duval you are partaking of the famous 'Duval Crawl' ('And bars to go before I sleep...'), and you will notice right off there is something here for everyone: fine restaurants, not so fine restaurants, T-shirt shops, strip clubs, semi-naked women ululating from second-floor balconies, gay bars, art galleries, cigar shops, T-shirts shops, illegal street performers, T-shirt shops, palm trees, time-share booths (masquerading as information booths), panhandlers, transients, did I mention

T-shirt shops? henna tattoo booths, pulsing music venues, restaurant touts, pedicabs, mopeds, pink taxis, a python wrangler, a bloke with an iguana on his shoulder (and iguana poop down his back) and a smiley chap on a push-bike who resembles a tanned Boris Johnson or Boomer Esiason.

Every conceivable square inch, every nook, every precious cranny, whether it be a crack between two buildings or simply an unused doorway, had a little flourishing business sprouting out of it. Talk about capitalism. We even saw a guy who had the world's smallest 'Cuban' cigar business protruding out from a set of steep stairs.

Key West is indeed more Caribbean than it is American. And like the Caribbean, it's a place you go to learn to scuba. And it's a place you go to enjoy tropical foliage, and island art and architecture. But it's also a place you go to get fucked up.

Duval Street was absolutely awash with paralytic revellers (walking about as sailors do on a rolling ship -- or on dry land, now that I think about it) and more of those Key West characters. Out in front of the Hog's Breath Saloon, and only about a block removed from Mallory Square, we happened upon an Ernest Hemingway-esque transient, with a lost-at-sea beard and hairy-knees, sitting on the curb. For some reason he seemed inordinately happy, in fact even happier than I am after the proctology exam is behind me for another year. Our Ernest was holding up a sign that read: 'Hell, why lie. I need some spare change so I can get drunk.'

We kept walking and passed by a shop with a sign in it that read: BUY ONE, GET THE SECOND ONE FREE! It was a shoe shop.

Then we saw someone who could have been Martha Stewart (or possibly the Widow Twanky) marching down the street. She was wearing a T-shirt that read: 'I have PMS and a gun. Excuse me, did you have something to say?'

In front of an entertainment complex called Rick's, a bony hand clamped on to my shoulder. I turned and stared into the wizened, weather-beaten face of someone I could only describe as a pirate -- a very polluted pirate (I'm a magnet to these people).

'Arrrghhh!' the pirate said. 'My name's Captain Jerry. I'm the Wizard of Key West. Say, my friend, can I borrow thirty-seven cents?'

I was so taken aback by the requested amount, I immediately forked over a dollar.

We plunged back into the river of overheated bodies (it looked as if a football match had just ended) and were immediately set upon by a wag in theatrical makeup who bore a striking resemblance to the Joker in *Batman*. To present an air of vaudeville, the Joker was wearing sandwich boards.

'Hi! I'm the Joke-Man,' he chortled. 'Wanna hear a joke? Only twenty-five cents?' Then, very deadpan, 'I've got cheaper ones, but they're not as funny.'

Gabrielle laughed and handed over a quarter. Anybody with this much determination deserved the custom.

'My wife and I divorced over religious differences,' the Joke-Man began, 'I thought I was God, but she didn't.' The Joke-Man laughed heartily at his own joke, then thanked us and accosted a family proudly wearing Green Bay Packer jerseys (away colours).

The crowd nudged us along at the speed continents shift. We peered into the window of a T-shirt shop. It featured T-shirts for infants. One T-shirt read: PARTY...MY CRIB...TWO A.M.

Laughing, we worked our way through an awful lot of people showing an awful lot of skin, up to the corner of Duval and Greene, and I thanked God we weren't going anywhere in a hurry. It was dark now and what a lovely night! Balmy, on the sticky side of muggy. Wind calm. Enormous moon rising. Heady aromas: night-blooming jasmine, bar smells, kitchen smells, body smells -- cannabis.

We stopped and looked kitty-corner across the street and right over there on the corner was none other than Sloppy Joe's bar (once the haunt of Ernest Hemingway). Just a block past Sloppy's, on the opposite side of the street, on the corner of Duval and Caroline, was a bar called the Bull & Whistle. The Bull & Whistle was an old wooden structure and it appeared to be made up of actually three bars: the 'Bull' on ground level, the 'Whistle' one flight up and the 'Garden of Eden' rooftop bar. The entire venue was old and funky and dark and moody, rough even, in an I'm-not-so-sure-I-will-come-out-alive sort of a way.

This was our kind of place!

We stepped out of the line of fire and gave the pub a good, hard look. All the windows were wide open and the joint was heaving. Up on stage, three forty-something women with beehive hairdos and squeezed into tight, silver sequined dresses were belting out *It's Raining Men*. Appropriate in a town with a large gay population. We were about to dive in when we spotted none other than Popcorn Joe. He was standing there on the corner with his mobile popcorn cart, working the Duval Street crowd.

We went up to Popcorn Joe. 'You were just at Mallory.'

'Very observant, masked man,' he said.

'How did you beat us here?'

Popcorn Joe placed his hands at his temples as a swami would: 'Let me guess. You took Duval, right?'

'Right.'

'Duval was sardine-city, so I took the alley.'

We hung out for a while and watched Popcorn Joe shovel popcorn and entertain the throngs. Joe seemed to know everyone on the street -- even the tourists. 'Hey, how ya doin', Woody? Nice to see ya again, ladies. Y'all stayin' long? Hope you left the kids at home.'

When there was a lull in the booming popcorn sales, I asked Popcorn Joe about the three women singing up on stage inside at the Bull.

'They're the Spectrelles. A Key West institution. Been around for ages.'

We listened as the Spectrelles sang *Y-M-C-A* (Gabrielle was miming the letters), then *Where the Boys Are*.

'Check out the bar on the top floor,' Joe suggested. 'You might find something of interest up there. Go around to the stairs on the side. You'll never make it if you try to storm the front.'

We went around the corner on Caroline Street, sent a cat screeching into the night, and took the wooden outside stairs up to the Whistle. We stuck our heads in and the place was mobbed with a cast of characters who looked as if they had just stepped out of a Patrick Swayse roadhouse movie. Good-natured drunks were shooting pool, shooting the shit and shooting Alabama Slammers. Some were even hanging over the Havana-influenced, wrap-around, wrought-iron balcony watching the world go by below on Duval.

Two puckish scamps had a fishing rod with a large hairy spider attached to the end of the fishing line, and they were finding it good sport to let it drop down on the unsuspecting tourists—usually female. We observed for a minute, saw them drop the hairy beast down, heard a cacophony of primordial screams from below, saw them quickly reel the spider back in. Then they cackled and toasted each other with Killian's Red.

Not wanting to be party to such frivolity (read: frightened of spiders), we fled up another flight of rickety stairs to the mysterious Garden of Eden rooftop bar.

'Check out the bar on the top floor,' Popcorn Joe had suggested. 'You might find something of interest up there.'

And you know what? Popcorn Joe was right. You see, the bar had a bouncer (the size of an American refrigerator) checking IDs, but that was not unusual, what was unusual was the bouncer was a woman, and she was wearing a string-bikini bottom -- that was really more like floss -- and she was topless. And she was pissed as a fiddler's bitch.

Gabrielle pushed me towards the bouncing bouncer and Miss Frigidaire greeted me in a somewhat erotic, rather rural

American I-can-suck-the-chrome-off-a-trailer-hitch manner and then gestured in the direction of the bar. How did this siren know that we suddenly needed a drink? A stiff one (I'm talking about the drink).

It was beyond dark up here in the Garden of Eden and when our eyes adjusted to the subdued lighting this is what we saw: We saw a young Cameron Diaz creature tending bar. She had false eyelashes like a Venus fly trap and was completely naked -- not even the floss -- and clearly a true blonde. And we spotted a DJ mixing tunes. He, too, was stark-buck naked. And we saw an artist. He was, get ready, *body* painting. And he apparently didn't want to get any paint on his clothes, because HE WASN'T WEARING ANY CLOTHES!!!

Neither did the guy who was having his body painted like a scene out of the original Garden of Eden, complete with the forked-tongue serpent. Or the bloke (hung like a racehorse) who was having his naked body painted like a pirate, replete with the golden dagger hanging from his sash.

East Renfrewshire this wasn't.

We peered into the dim light and cringed. Out on a dance floor, naked merrymakers were dancing to a very hump-me beat of a not-so-refined nature. In the wings, topless women, naked men and a few professional voyeurs of indeterminate sex were whacking back the bevy.

Key West was the epicentre of debauchery!

'Been to America before,' Gabrielle shouted over the music. 'Wasn't like this at the Magic Kingdom.'

'They're having one helluva party down here and the rest of the world doesn't know it's going on.'

The pirate/stud horse paid the body painter and hoofed it to the dance floor. I threw myself in front of Gabrielle to protect her so she wouldn't get accidentally flogged by Long Schlong Silver -- then I ordered a Budweiser and a margarita from Cameron Diaz behind the b-b-b-bar. Up close,

Cameron had a rough look, but it was softened by a syrupy, seminal, phone-sex voice.

The feeling up here was one of being very far removed from the real world, the perfect place to come on holiday if you felt the need to get your mind off the backstabbing at work, the depressing side effects of your depression medication or that £80 parking ticket.

I inhaled my beer. And Gabrielle threw down her margarita. Then we did the same thing all over again. We were too embarrassed to stay -- and too embarrassed to leave.

Now what! A thundering commotion over by the bouncer suddenly rumbled our way. A group of young gays, naked except for G-strings and runners, had their bodies painted like zebras. They were coming in for a touchup -- and possibly a blow dry.

Jet lag was kicking in. We needed to go back to the hotel, but how were we going to escape from this bar? Perhaps we would make a move when the herd of zebras kicked up their heels.

CHAPTER 2

A parrot with red and green feathers was peeping at me from a mango tree just outside our window when I awoke the next morning.

I watched the parrot watching me, then turned my attention to the ceiling fan circling lazily above our bed. Round and round and round. In my addled state of consciousness, the ceiling fan became a hamster wheel.

What should we do? What would you do? Should we jump off the hamster wheel?

The capricious notion of chucking caution directly into the face of the prevailing westerlies and seeing if we could survive in Key West had wreaked havoc with my sleep and I had had certifiable dreams. Dreams of being stuck on the Kingston Bridge, surrounded by incensed drivers. And I recognised many of the angry faces: my boss at the airport, my mum-in-law, and Glasgow Councillor George Redmond. George Redmond was cajoling us back: 'Ye wonnae find a good curry over there, laddie!'

The parrot squawked me back to reality and dampened, well, soaked, last night's enthusiasm. If we wanted to stay, we needed to find jobs -- and fast. We simply didn't have the funds to weather a protracted job search and house hunt.

And the clock was ticking. We had a six-day window before our return flight to Glasgow.

The first issue on the agenda was to escape from this pricey hotel. Upon arrival from Miami the previous day, we'd booked the first hotel we saw without shopping around. If we were going to make a move it had to be now.

When I rolled over to see if Gabrielle was awake, and then rolled over again (king-sized bed), I saw my wife sitting at the little desk in our room, pouring through the Yellow Pages.

'Doing some leisure reading?' I croaked.

'Looking for a short-stay apartment so we can move out of the hotel. Oh, here's one. The Pineapple Guest House. They rent by the night, week, month or season. Reckon it will be cheaper to stay there until we find jobs.'

Ah, my wife.

'And the guest house is only two blocks removed from our beloved Bull & Whistle pub.'

My brilliant wife.

* * *

We rang the guest house, but there was no answer, so we decided to see if we could find it. We quickly showered, dressed and went to check out. A leafy path led us to a secluded swimming pool set in a small jungle.

'Look!' Gabrielle whispered.

'Look at what?' I whispered back.

'The people on the sunbeds!'

I had a peep and my eyeballs sprang out of my head. Everyone was naked -- and frying. Some were sunny side up. Others over easy. Then the handyman strolled down the path and he too was naked except for the tool belt.

What kind of hotel was this?

At reception I rang a bell and out popped a young goddess. She presented us with a big smile and that was all she was wearing. She, too, was in the buff. I handed back the key and the receptionist/goddess jiggled off in to a back room (and I swear I heard the sound of a bongo drum as she went).

'How do you apply for this kind of job?' Gabrielle whispered. 'You can't exactly send in your CV.'

'Perhaps she just turned up and showed her credentials.'

'She certainly has those.'

We picked up one of the hotel's brochures and studied it. It laid bare the naked truth: The hotel was a 'clothing-optional' hotel.

Did anyone in Key West wear clothes?

We rented bicycles from a man in shorts but no shirt at a place around the corner frighteningly called the Moped Hospital, then secured our lone holdall in my bike's basket and set off down Duval Street to find the Pineapple Guest House.

It was only ten o'clock in the morning, yet it was startlingly hot and humid. What would it be like in the height of summer?

We pedalled on and saw a rusty, old pickup truck with a bumper sticker that read: KEY WEST, A DRINKING TOWN WITH A TOURIST PROBLEM.

Key West by day looked so different: a little hung over, a little weather-beaten and a bit worn around the edges -- very laid-back and very artsy -- and there were cats everywhere.

We heard as many conversations in Spanish, as in English. And we saw a funeral procession, on foot, pass by: men in black trousers and white shirts, women in fancy white dresses and white gloves. A trumpet was being played as mourners shuffled sombrely in time to the music. Our trusty guidebook told us that the cemetery was located in the dead centre of the Old Town ever since an 1847 hurricane had disinterred bodies from the original cemetery, which had been located less than a block from the sea. We followed the procession at a discreet distance and when the column moved off to a far section of the cemetery, we took a little turn around the graveyard on our bikes.

Key West is a coral island and the coral is virtually impenetrable. Can you guess what this means? All the 'graves' in the cemetery are *above* ground. We found vaults and mausoleums and headstones leaning at wonky angles. And we unearthed, even here in the cemetery, Key West's playful spirit and quirky sense of humour. Inscribed on the facing tablet of a large white crypt was 'I TOLD YOU I WAS SICK'. And not far away, on a different tomb, 'DEVOTED FAN OF JULIO IGLESIAS'. And on yet another, obviously inscribed by some poor sod's widow, 'AT LEAST I KNOW WHERE HE'S SLEEPING TONIGHT'.

We fled the cemetery and wound our way an immemorable route through lush back alleys and tropical lanes and spilled out on to Elizabeth Street. We passed the library on the corner of Elizabeth and Fleming, carried on for a block, turned right on Eaton and then coasted gently down a narrow passage called Peacon Lane that was filled with ramshackle cottages, tropical flowers and the fragrance of frangipani.

It smacked of a bygone era back here, and I was in the process of setting my watch back 50 years when we noticed something and screeched our Schwinns to a halt. Down at the end of Peacon Lane, a bloke resembling Elvis Costello was hunched over a mobile pushcart. It was Popcorn Joe. He had three cats milling about beneath his feet and he was working in an open garage door, cleaning his Pretty Good Popcorn cart.

'You're everywhere!' I said, as we pulled up.

Joe laughed. 'Key West is like that. If you can't find somebody you're looking for, jump on your bike and tool around the Old Town.' A reflective beat. 'And if you're trying to avoid someone, good luck!'

'Are those your cats?' Gabrielle asked.

'Yup. All three: Chubba, B.C. and Scaredy-cat.'

Then Popcorn Joe asked: 'What did you think of the Garden of Eden?'

'Colourful,' Gabrielle said. 'I felt like a bit of a scaredy-cat.'

Popcorn Joe laughed again. We liked this guy.

'By the way, could you tell us how to get to the Pineapple Guest House, please?'

Joe pointed to a motorcycle parked in front of a wooden gate a few feet away. The wooden gate led to a tropical compound beyond. 'Other side of that Hawg. Are you looking for a room?'

'Is this your place?'

'Yeah, my wife Clara and I've had it for about fifteen years.'

'Thought you sold popcorn?'

'Do that, too. That's Key West. You do whatever the heck you like here. No one cares, usually.' Then: 'Wait till you meet Roger. He lives in one of the apartments. He's from Seattle. His wife had it up to here with him and booted him out, so he escaped down to Key West. Wanted to get as far away from her as he could. He used to be a stockbroker, but here he drives a taxi. He doesn't make much money, doesn't own anything, doesn't have any credit cards and finally he's found happiness.'

Popcorn Joe's cell phone rang. He answered: 'How much? I think I can swing that. Two people, seven nights...'

So that's what it was all about.

A noise behind us. A squeaky, rusty bike pulled up and we turned to behold a bare-chested cur, with an I've-been-sniffing-too-much-glue smile, straddling his bike. It was the Fish-Man from Mallory Square, and he had a beaten-up wheelie bin attached to the back of his bicycle.

'Help yourself, Fish-Man,' Popcorn Joe said, then he turned towards us. 'I'll put you upstairs so you can sit out on the balcony. Let me go grab you a key.'

Popcorn Joe split stage right and we watched as Fish-Man climbed off his bike, rooted through one of Popcorn Joe's rubbish bins and scooped out handful after handful of popcorn.

'Popcorn Joe dumps all the stale popcorn in the trash, then I come here the next morning and snag it for my fish.'

Fish-Man leaned close and said conspiratorially: 'Popcorn Joe and I, we have a symbiotic relationship. One man's trash is another man's chum.'

And on that, Fish-Man glanced at the sky, announced that it was going to rain, mounted his bike with a beaten-up wheelie bin attached to the back and pedalled off.

We looked about. It was so peaceful here. The sun was hot on our faces. Large cumulus clouds shifted lazily overhead. A rainbow shimmered in the distance. Living in Key West was living in a picture postcard -- albeit with tattered edges.

Something caught my eye. I pointed to a small brass sign embedded in the corner of Popcorn Joe's building. It said: ON THIS SITE, IN 1984, NOTHING HAPPENED.

We both laughed out loud.

Key West had character -- and characters, lots of them -- and it was startlingly refreshing.

Popcorn Joe returned with our key.

'Need a deposit?' I asked.

'What for, in case you steal the building? C'mon, let's bolt. It's gonna rain.'

And then it did indeed start to rain, and I mean rain, a real tropical torrential downpour and more water fell from the heavens than we thought was physically possible. And it looked as if it would never stop.

It lasted ten minutes.

And then the sun came back out.

* * *

It's late in the afternoon now and we're at the Bull & Whistle having a coffee. Even by day the air in this drinkery hangs heavy with decadence and end-of-the-world intrigue. We think the female bartender is already pissed.

At the end of the bar we find a lonely copy of the local daily newspaper, the Key West *Citizen*. We turn to the

Classifieds and peruse the columns for Apartment Rentals and our mouths drop open. Something quickly becomes crystal clear: We will never be able to afford to live in Key West. A modest one-bedroom flat is going for at least $1000, and two-bedroom flats are $1500 and up. Way up. First month's rent, last month's rent and a security deposit equal to a month's rent (in case we steal the building) have to be paid up front. On top of that, we have to fork over deposits for electricity, garbage, and water and sewer. And even cable for the TV (if you want to receive any programmes in English). Just to get into a simple one-bedroom apartment we will have to lay out well over $3000.

I turn the page and read on, and as I do I start to read between the lines. Some places have hardwood floors (which sounds very attractive and translates to 'cool floor in warm climate'), other places have ceiling fans (which can mean 'tropical elegance', but more than likely means 'no air conditioning'), and yet other places offer 'off-street parking' (which means, if this is not mentioned, the flat or cottage you may find will have no available parking this side of Miami Beach).

Gabrielle is reading over my shoulder. 'This is a nightmare, these prices. Wait! What about that one?'

OLD TOWN -- Furnished Efficiency. Very private area, ceiling fans, no smokers, no pets, no drugs, no parties, no parking. $975 month, F/L/S (First, Last, Security). Good credit and references.

'That one's out,' I say. 'We don't have any references.'

We turn to the next ad:

OLD TOWN -- 35' Fiberglass Houseboat. 6-cylinder. Mercruiser Diesel, New Holding Tank and AC's. Top, Fwd and Aft Decks. Pet OK. $1500/mo. F/L/S.

'A houseboat sounds great.'

'It says "Pet OK". We could have a catfish.'

'Or a dogfish.'

'Parrot fish.'

'Seahorse.'

We move down the page to the next ad:

OLD TOWN -- Treetop Paradise Living w/ 300 sq. ft. deck, overlooking heated pool on beautiful compound grounds. Newly renovated, delightfully appointed, custom office. Great for executive or writer. F/L/S, $2,000 mo.

'Oh, yeah, we'll take that one. When can we move in?'

'It doesn't even mention anything about how many bedrooms or if it has A/C.'

Next ad:

NEW TOWN -- Gorgeous, renovated studio cottage. Everything new, private landscaped yard, carport, $1150/mo. Water, sewer, elec, cable TV extra. F/L/S. Quiet tenants only. No parties. Small pet negotiable.

'Small pet negotiable?' Gabrielle says. 'What is that supposed to mean? Sounds as if they're into *Santería*.'

'Oh, wait, here's one. This place has our name written all over it.'

PRIVATE ISLAND -- Off Big Pine Key, sandy beach, towering palms, lush tropical jungle. 2BR/2BA Old historic lodge filled with sea memorabilia, antiques, large library, vast decks and porches facing Looe Key National Park Reef. Boat dockage on Big Pine, about 1½ miles to island. $3,950/mo.

'And only just out of our price range.'

'And the sea memorabilia was such a draw.'

To make a long boring story, a short boring story, we perused the Apartment Rentals further and the Voice of Doom was narrating the Classifieds now. We were in trouble.

Gabrielle and I put down the paper and discussed the larcenous rates, the extortionate rents, the silly deposits, the limited choices (at least for us). And I could tell by my wife's body language that the high cost of living was not exactly making her day.

'We're going to find a way to make this work,' I said. 'We Breakfields are not quitters. You watch. We're going to land on our feet.'

On this, an older well-dressed gentleman sitting at the bar next to us -- who smelled lightly of Tequila -- leaned over and said: 'Excuse me, I couldn't help but overhear. Are you looking for a place? I rent apartments here on the island.'

'We're looking,' I said. 'But we're being blinded by reality.'

'Here's my card,' he said. 'I work for a real estate company. I'm sure we can find something for you.'

I looked at the man's card. It said Ben Correador – CAROLINE STREET REALTY.

We introduced ourselves and then sat there -- all ears -- as Ben told us how we could bypass the standard first month, last month and security deposit palaver. 'You simply pay the first month's rent and back up your commitment with a credit card. You do have a credit card, don't you?'

A credit card was the one thing we did possess, albeit with a humiliatingly low limit.

'If you've got time now, I could show you some places. I don't have the keys to any of the apartments with me, but you could at least see if you like the location.'

Well, we couldn't believe our good fortune. I had told Gabrielle we were going to land on our feet, but even I didn't expect to plant them on terra firma Cayo Hueso quite so quickly.

Ben had his car parked around the corner. The car was a bit trashed for a successful estate agent. 'This is a loaner,' Ben told us. 'Caddie's in the shop. Next time we'll ride in luxury.'

The first place Ben showed us was a one-bedroom flat on Fleming Street. It was on the second floor, and we could see that it had ceiling fans, A/C and a small balcony. The price was fourteen-hundred dollars per month and it was unfurnished.

Ben said he needed to call the office, so while he was on his cell phone, Gabrielle and I discussed the balcony flat.

'I like the location,' Gabrielle said, 'but I think we need to find a flat that's furnished. And less expensive.'

When Ben finished with his call, we asked him if he had anything furnished.

'I've got loads of places,' he said. 'C'mon, let's go find exactly what you're looking for.'

The next place we looked at was on the other side of the island, but in Key West the 'other side of the island' is not very far away. As the apartment was on the ground floor, we could see through the windows. It was light and airy, with A/C and hardwood floors. The price twelve-hundred a month.

'Anything cheaper?' Gabrielle asked.

Ben drove back into the Old Town and showed us a flat in an old Victorian house around the corner from the Key West library. It was on the ground floor and had a porch up front and a small deck out back. Since I live in libraries, we felt this was an ideal location.

'The tenants don't move out until the day after tomorrow,' Ben told us, as we peered in the windows. 'But all that rattan furniture stays, and that deep-pile shag goes. The owner is installing hardwood floors. Why don't we set up a time so you can see it after they've vacated the premises? We'll just need a few days to get it ready.'

Gabrielle and I were seriously interested.

'How much?' I asked.

'A thousand a month.'

'That place is only a thousand?'

'And the utilities are included,' Ben added.

I gave Gabrielle a look and her eyes were glowing. 'And if we use the credit card as a deposit, we don't have to put out any more cash up front?'

'Only if you want to buy me a beer,' Ben joked.

We all laughed. If we could get this place, we'd buy Ben all the beer he wanted.

As we stood there, admiring the surrounding palm trees and conch gingerbread trim, a car pulled up and a couple scrambled out. The couple stood for a moment reading house numbers, then they pointed to 'our' flat, hurried up and put their noses to the windows.

'Can I help you?' Ben asked.

'Caroline Street Realty sent us over to look at this apartment.'

I shot Ben a look and he flashed back a big reassuring smile.

'Sorry, folks, but these people were here first.'

Then he took Gabrielle and me aside.

'Listen, I saw these two in the office earlier. They're hot to trot. If you want this place, it's yours. I'd put down a deposit to hold it if I were you.'

'How much?' I asked.

'I'd do the full thousand.'

'I'll give it to you right now,' I said. 'You take traveller's cheques?'

'Anything negotiable,' Ben joked.

As I was signing the cheques -- on Gabrielle's back -- I glanced over at the couple who had just lost this place, and they were shooting daggers our way.

'Snowbirds,' Ben whispered.

I handed Ben ten traveller's cheques and whispered back: 'More like vultures.'

'Timing is everything,' Ben laughed. 'I'm going to get them out of our hair.'

Ben went to the couple-from-hell and told them about the apartments that we had just seen and that seemed to placate them. Then he came back over to us.

'You were right. Vultures. But I got them all calmed down. Let me show them an apartment or two and then I'll meet you over at Caroline Street Reality. Would you believe it's on Caroline?

'We're staying on Caroline!' I said.

'Great. Meet me there in half-an-hour and we'll sign all the papers, and I'll get your credit card info. Then the first beer's on me.'

We watched Ben load the vultures into his rent-a-wreck and then we walked -- with a bounce in our step, might I add -- over to Caroline Street Reality -- on Caroline. And guess what? It was almost across the street from the Pineapple Guest House. This is always happening to me. Something is right in front of my eyes and it takes me days to notice it. I guess this is why I didn't get hired on when they had that opening with Air Traffic Control.

Gabrielle and I stepped into the cool, air-conditioned confines of Caroline Street Reality and an immensely pleasant woman greeted us. If everyone in Key West was as amiable as Ben and this woman, we were really going to enjoy living here.

'Hi. Can I help you?' she asked, and gave us a lots-of-time-spent-in-the-dentist's-chair smile.

'We're waiting for Ben. We're supposed to meet here.'

'I'll go get him for you,' the receptionist said. 'Have a seat.'

'He's back already?'

Nod of the head. Lots of perfect teeth.

There was a magazine sitting on a coffee table called GREAT HOMES YOU'LL NEVER BE ABLE TO AFFORD IN PARADISE, or something like that, so Gabrielle and I poured through the glossy pages and peered at all the glorious homes that only people in glossy-paged magazines seem to own. But who cared? So we would never be able to afford a villa on the beach with a swimming pool and cathedral ceilings and a master bedroom the size of a squash court. The place Ben had found for us was idyllic. And we couldn't believe it. We were going to land on our feet after all and our feet were going to be living in Key West, Florida, not-quite-the USA!

'And how can I be of help to you?' came a friendly voice.

Gabrielle and I looked up to see an elderly well-dressed man standing in front of us.

'We're waiting to see Ben Correador,' I said.

'I'm Ben Correador.'

I looked over at Gabrielle and then back at the man. The rug -- a deep-pile shag -- had just been pulled out from under our once happy feet.

* * *

A thousand dollars may not dent the coffers of some people, but it was a big chunk to us. And it hurt. And we were deeply embarrassed.

If you promise not to tell anyone, I'll just mention, sotto voce, that we were victims of a similar con in Tenerife. The amount of money we'd lost was considerably less, although the result was equally humiliating. In my enthusiasm to surprise my wife with my sense of adventure, I had booked an exotic day trip with a Thomson rep on a moped -- who wasn't a Thomson rep. Just a fast moped driver.

How soon we get old, how late we get smart.

And, yes, we did telephone the Key West police. And you know what? Do you know how this great protector of man and beast responded? They wouldn't take the report. That's right. Their reasoning? Anyone that brain-dead deserved what they got. And their final words to us? 'Welcome to Key West.'

Welcome, indeed.

* * *

Gabrielle and I went back to the Bull and asked the now palatic bartender if she had ever seen the older man before, and she slurred: 'Never seen the two of you before.'

We were going nowhere -- other than back to East Sussex. We had been in town less than twenty-four hours and had already 'spent' over twelve-hundred dollars. I flipped through our remaining traveller's cheques. Then I flipped through them all over again. Even a mathematically challenged bloke could do the math. We didn't have enough funds left to last the week.

Depressed and bewildered, we hung out at the Bull a little while longer and shared a small fizzy water. We decided to wait until the masses commenced their pilgrimage down towards Mallory and the setting sun. As the bewitching hour approached, we noticed something strange (in a day already filled with strange). Everyone was coming from Mallory Square, not going to it. Why did the rest of the world always seem to know something we didn't?

We took off down Duval, past Sloppy Joe's, Rum Runner's, the Hog's Breath. All these pubs were full. Why weren't people spilling out and making their way to the Sunset Celebration? When we rounded the corner and saw Mallory Square straight in front of us, we stopped dead in our flippies. So this was the problem: A towering cruise ship was docked at Mallory Dock and it had obliterated the setting sun.

And vendors and performers and minstrels and troubadours were livid.

We spotted Popcorn Joe leaning against his popcorn cart.

'How's business?'

'Nonexistent. That cruise ship was supposed to be out of here well before sunset. No sunset, no tourists, no biz.' Then: 'Are you all settled in at the guest house?'

'Yes, we are, thanks,' Gabrielle said. 'Love the banana trees.'

'Have you met the others yet?' Popcorn Joe asked. 'There's Roger who I told you about, a divorcee with three screaming kids, a chick who drove her Harley down from Alabama and two nuns. The nuns come every year.'

'Nuns come to Key West?'

'It's an incongruous image, isn't it? Say, why don't we meet for a beer later at the Bull. I'm treating...' Popcorn Joe looked around at the lack of tourists, '...if I make any money, that is.'

'You're on,' I said. Popcorn Joe was having a bad day, as well, but he was commendably upbeat and it made us feel a little better.

We headed down to the other end of Mallory Dock where the tightrope walker was mooning the rich folk up on the promenade deck of the cruise ship.

About now, a man dressed in an orange boilersuit (similar to the dress code in American prisons) and a baseball cap yelled at me from a distance: 'Hey, you! Yes, *you*! We gotta get this cruise ship out of here before sunset. Give me a hand. Help me untie it.'

Well, what luck! Perhaps if I made a good impression I'd get offered a job working on the docks. 'Tell me what to do!' I shouted back to the crew member.

'You untie the stern! I'll get the bow! C'mon. Move! Move! Move!'

'Aye, aye!' I shouted.

This unforeseen opportunity provided us with an emotional lift, so Gabrielle went off to procure alcohol, and I tore into my task with unbridled zest. And just so you know, untying a cruise ship is not the easiest thing to do. These are big beasts. And the bloody ropes are as thick as your thigh. But I gave the hemp the ol' heave-ho and was pretty proud of my effort. Yes, I was pretty proud as I watched the stern of that mighty cruise ship as it was sucked slowly away from the dock by the outgoing tide and what joy when I saw the oppressive gloom of the shadows disappear and be replaced by the golden rays of the setting sun!

I heard wild cheers and applause. All the vendors and crafts people on the dock were going nuts. Were they acknowledging me? Had I in some small way done something to rescue the little people? Had I helped save their livelihood? Had something finally gone right?

I waved at all my newfound friends, saw Popcorn Joe in the background (for some unknown reason with a look of horror on his face), and that's when I felt the bony hand on my shoulder. It must be Captain Jerry, the Wizard of Key West, there to congratulate me for my deed (or ask me for thirty-seven cents) -- but it wasn't, rather it was a fairly impressive contingency from the Key West Police Department.

'What in the goddamn hell do you think you're doing, ass-fuck?' one of them bellowed in my face.

'Untying the cruise ship!' I offered in my defence, and that's when I saw a bloke in an orange boilersuit being led away in handcuffs. 'He asked me to help him! That guy over there! He's crew!'

'He's not crew shit-for-brains. That's Fish-Man. You're under arrest.'

And as I was being hauled off by the fearless Key West police, I saw Gabrielle round the corner carrying two, tall, cool drinks with little umbrellas sticking out the top.

* * *

Later that night Gabrielle and I were sitting at the bar in the Bull. Gabrielle was watching the spitting-image of Charlotte Church dip Oreo cookies into Tequila. I was thanking Popcorn Joe with Budweisers (which were astonishingly cold) for keeping my hide out of the slammer. I now owed Popcorn Joe 'free beer for life', you see, Popcorn Joe just happened to know all the cops in the Key West Police Department and that simple fact had saved my touron-arse.

We sipped our beer and watched as a Budweiser truck pulled up out front.

'They're delivering beer at this time of night?' I asked.

'It's a thirsty town,' Popcorn Joe said knowingly.

We observed as the Budweiser truck driver and his partner, a strapping young lad, unloaded keg after keg of beer and hurried them in a side door.

On this Popcorn Joe waved a hand in the air and yelled over to the bartender: 'Another round of Bud, please!'

We watched the beer being loaded and drank our beers.

Popcorn Joe ordered us yet another round: 'Two more, please!'

We turned our attention back to the two men unloading the beer. They were now drenched in sweat and really hopping to it. And this is when Popcorn Joe turned to me, gestured for me to drink and said: 'Hurry up. They're gaining on us!'

We had a good laugh, then told Popcorn Joe about our wild, romantic scheme of not going home and how it had all fallen apart. And do you know what Popcorn Joe said?

'If you're interested, I've been looking for a couple to manage the guest house. Can't seem to find anyone responsible.'

'How do you know we're responsible?'

'You showed up at the bar on time.' Then: 'You can live upstairs in the attic. There's a small apartment up there. The ceiling is low. You'd have to bend over a lot, but the rent's free.'

CHAPTER 3

Key West is not known for its great beaches.

Bournemouth, with its seven miles of rich golden sand has vastly superior beaches (and better beer) than Key West. You see, Key West's problem is all that coral.

When you stroll along the beach in, say, Brighton, you are at least walking on those smooth, bagel-like stones. When you stroll on a beach in Key West, you are walking on the marine equivalent of broken glass.

Natural deep-sand beaches are nonexistent in Key West, but one beach, Smathers Beach, does have sand, although it's imported. Here you can frolic about, play volleyball and Frisbee, but the minute you step off that cushion of artificial cat-litter and stick but one toe in the inviting bath-like sea, you step into oceanic hell. Bathers in the know wear those diving booties or they keep their flippies on or they simply avoid bathing. If you are easily bored -- and a bit twisted -- and want to see some lively action, ride your bicycle out to Smathers Beach and watch all the unsuspecting tourists take their first step into the briny, spiny sea (I speak from experience here).

The Pier House Resort, down by the glass-bottom boat at the foot of Duval, has a small four-star manmade beach with a not-very-secluded topless section. And this is a great place to sneak into and swim and gawp -- if you don't mind being sucked out halfway to Cuba when the vicious tide ebbs. This lively area has buoys and ropes, and more than once we saw stranded, frightened bathers (with stiff necks and erections) hanging on to the buoys for dear life as the outgoing tide tried to dampen their holiday.

Higgs Beach, just this side of the White Street Pier and the AIDS Memorial, has a sprinkling of natural sand and this is where locals hang out, so you can imagine it's undeniably colourful here. And it's a good place to splash about and snorkel if you don't mind returning to your towel from a reviving dip in the Atlantic only to find that your towel is missing, along with all personal items -- including that last sachet of Resolve (I speak from experience here).

Bournemouth has a KidZone scheme, Key West has a CrimeZone scene.

So this is why Gabrielle and I are now baking in the hot sun at Fort Zachary Taylor. Fort Zack, as it's known, is a State Park. We had to pay a modest fee to gain entry, but it's well worth it. Sort of the American equivalent of a Blue Flag beach.

Fort Zack also has some engaging history: A Cuban family, desperate to escape from the repressive rule of Castro and realize their dream of free elections and freedom of expression, climbed onboard a derelict sailboat and aimed for America. Not having any experience on the High Seas, the Cuban family drifted aimlessly in the Florida Straits for five days at the mercy of the powerful Gulf Stream. They were out of water and drinking their own urine, which I guess is not unlike drinking some American beer. The frightened family tried navigating with a small corroded compass, but try as they might to head north, the powerful Gulf Stream had other plans. The family didn't possess a torch so at night to consult their compass they had to illuminate the instrument by holding up a small glass jar filled with fire flies they had captured back home in *La Habana*.

On the sixth day the seas grew angry during the dead middle of the night. Everyone was afraid they would capsize and drown. Just when the family was about to give up hope of surviving, let alone reaching America and freedom, one of the children suddenly pointed and shouted: '*Mira! Mira!* America!' Though just a boy, the young lad had spotted that great red and white symbol of America -- the brightly illuminated Coca Cola machine at the concession stand on the beach at Fort Zachary Taylor.

Amazing story, I thought, then I turned and looked back at that very soda machine. And it gave me goose pimples -- on a day when the temperature was soaring up close to 80 degrees.

We took a dip in the inviting ocean. It was mind-boggling to think Havana was just out there! We splashed about. The water was startlingly warm, even for January. And clear. We could see parrot fish and small barracudas and sand crabs and even tiny black-and-yellow striped Sergeant Majors that kept darting between our legs.

We dripped back to our towels -- which were still there -- slapped on more BullFrog SPF 45 sunblock and picked up the books we were currently reading (Gabrielle and I usually tried to read each other's book -- not concurrently, mind you -- so we could discuss them, shiver over the drama and rejoice in the comedy).

This was indeed paradise here. And so tranquil. Fleecy racks of clouds drifted overhead. Shrimp boats bobbed on the horizon. And charter fishing boats chugged back in from the reef.

We read a little and talked a lot about staying in Key West. That's right, we hadn't given Popcorn Joe an answer yet. The minute Joe had presented us with the offer, reality slapped us across the face, and hard. And now we were weighing the consequences: Would we miss our Second City of the

Empire? Yes. Would we miss struggling to access the Buchanan Galleries carpark at Christmas? No. Would we miss Wednesday Curry Night with Planky and Steve down the pub? Yes. Would we miss our neighbours, the 'plate-tists', who felt it necessary to own a car so new the paint wasn't even dry yet? No. Would we miss our verdant parks, sidewalk cafés and shopping on Buchanan Street? Yes. Would we miss the litter that swirls in and around every public place, including, sadly, our verdant parks, sidewalk cafés and Buchanan Street? No.

But there was family to consider. And then there was the UK. We loved everything about it -- except perhaps a few fringe royals.

We watched the biplane cruise by. Read some more. Spied an elderly fisherman casting off the end of the breakwater. Saw gay couples sunning in the lee of that same breakwater. Followed a shapely lass windsurfing. Everybody seemed to be accepted here.

Still in a quandary, Gabrielle and I dived back into our books and were submerged for quite some time (I was reading about Bill Bryson walking through Weston-super-Mare at six o'clock on a Tuesday evening. 'The streets were empty, dark, and full of slanting rain...')

'What day is it today?' I asked Gabrielle.

'Tuesday.'

'And what time is it?'

'Dunno. Late in the afternoon. Could be five or six.'

'And we're sitting on a pristine beach with Cuba and all its intrigue just over the horizon?'

'Right.'

'And our faces look like lobsters?'

'Right.'

'And we've got lovely, painful sunburns on just one side of our legs?'

'Right.'

'And when the cold front that's forecast comes through tonight, it's going to drop no lower than the mid-sixties?'

'Right.'

Gabrielle put down her book and a smile as wide as the crescent-shaped beach we were sitting on crossed her face.

'We're not going back, are we?'

'Right!' I said.

And then we just sat there for a long while, tingling with the excitement that comes from doing something daring and adventurous in life -- and just a little bit misguided -- but most of all for wrestling control of our lives.

* * *

'Hey, dude and dudette!' A rough voice, that could only emanate from the tobacco chewing mouth of a Hell's Angel, snapped us out of our reverie of relocating to Key West.

We looked up and saw a deeply tanned bloke, built like a brick shithouse, casting a shadow on us. He was dripping with tattoos and seawater and he had green, homemade flippers attached to his hands.

'Hi! I'm Shark-Man,' he announced. 'Saw you reading that book. What's it called?'

'*Notes from a Small Island*,' I said.

'Any good?'

'A stonking good read,' I said.

'Stonking?' Shark-Man said.

'You'll find yourself laughing out loud in public places,' I said, and handed him the book.

Shark-Man studied the cover, smiled, flipped the book over and read the blurb on the back jacket, then read the first page: 'Cool!' Shark-Man said, 'I'll have to see if I can get it.'

'If you don't mind me asking,' I said, knowing that he was dying for me to ask, 'Why are you called "Shark-Man"?'

'Glad you asked!' he said. 'I swim with sharks. If I hear there's been a sighting, I dive right into the water and go looking for the shark.'

'There's sharks right out there!' Gabrielle gasped.

Shark-Man gave her a great big *Jaws* smile: 'Shit-loads.'

We watched as a small commuter aircraft, arriving from Miami, banked just offshore and swung back towards the island.

'More snowbirds arriving,' Shark-Man noted. 'This is high season here, now. They all come down from the North and drink Duval dry.' Then a look of horror on his face: 'Say, you're not from the great white North, are you?'

'No, the UK.'

Shark-Man studied us for a moment. 'Well, shit on me. That's why you said "stonking". I knew you were from somewhere. Welcome.' Then: 'We like the Brits here. If it wasn't for you we'd all be speaking Spanish!'

Gabrielle and I laughed -- and we were touched.

Nosy is not good, curious with tact is acceptable (not that I have any tact): 'So then, is being Shark-Man a vocation or avocation?'

Shark-Man gave us a look of 'What the fuck?'

'Occupation or hobby,' Gabrielle clarified.

'Well, it would be both, then. It's what I like and it's what I do. I'm crew on a yacht. Owned by a big multimillionaire crazy sumbitch. He owns newspapers. Had a shark cage built and wanted someone to look after him when he was down there taking photos and scaring the crap out of his snobby guests. He put an ad in the Mullet Wrap. The Mullet Wrap is what we locals call the daily newspaper. It's not known for its reporting -- or spelling for that matter -- so we've named it the Mullet Wrap because that's all it's good for.'

Shark-Man smiled, then became reflective: 'Don't think my boss owns that newspaper so it must have pissed him off royally to have to pay for a classified.'

Shark-Man laughed at his own insight, then followed a seabird as it dived into the near-shore waters for a fishy morsel.

'Anyway, he put an ad in the paper. Had his yacht anchored out by the reef. A lot of people applied for the job:

marine biologists, professional fishermen, certified divers, y'know, real folk.'

'You got the job and all those qualified people didn't?' I asked.

'Yeah, I charmed the shit out of that rich sumbitch. A dude who's seen it all.'

'How'd you manage that?' Gabrielle said.

'I swam out to apply. He gave me the job right then and there. Said I was his man.' Then: 'Shoulda seen the look on his face when I came crawling up over the stern of his yacht wearing these green homemade flippers on my hands.'

We laughed. Shark-Man was not the type of guy you wanted to meet anywhere near a dark alley, but he was exceedingly likable in broad daylight.

A blur on the horizon breached our attention. We froze and watched as a dark speck became an approaching aircraft. It was closing -- and fast.

'The hell's going on?' Shark-Man said. 'That motherfucker's way too low.'

The plane was skimming the ocean. We heard the rumble of its engines as it approached, then WHOOOSH!!! it skimmed right overhead, almost clipping the tree tops. It was a fighter jet and it was all black with a red star painted on its tail.

'Cuban MiG!' Shark-Man yelled. 'Take cover!'

The after-roar was deafening. We thought we were being invaded.

'Holy shit!' Shark-Man added.

Everyone on the beach was confused and shaken.

'Give me the sharks, any day,' Shark-Man said. 'That scared the shit out of me.'

'Took the words right out of my mouth,' Gabrielle said, with her hands still over her ears.

We all blew out our cheeks, then Shark-Man's eyes dilated balefully. A cacophony of evil was approaching from the opposite side of the island. A frightening wail grew like an imminent tornado. Sunbathers scattered as the MiG blowtorched the trees from the other direction, roared out to sea, kicked in the afterburners, then banked sharply left and punched out black plumes of fiery exhaust.

'Our one-man invasion force is heading for Boca Chica!' Shark-man yelled. 'That's the Naval Air Station on a neighbouring key.'

I looked at Shark-Man and he stared back at me with eyes as big as jellyfish. 'I'm going back in the water where it's safe!' And then he was gone, back to the safety of the warm shark-infested coastal waters of the Florida Keys.

I glanced at my wife. And Gabrielle uttered 'Holy Shit!' Just like Shark-Man. And I pretty much felt that summed up my sentiments, as well.

CHAPTER 4

It's geography time.

Yes, time has come for me to draw you a sophisticated, yet edible, map. Okay, take that curry you're stuffing your face with and place the entire dish in the middle of the table -- don't forget the poppadums. The plate of curry represents the round, bottom half of the state of Florida. Now take a poppadum and break it up into a whole lot of little pieces of various sizes. Take those pieces and place one right beneath your curry dish. This is Key Largo. Now sprinkle the rest out in a long chain to your left. These are the Florida Keys. Put down as many pieces as you want. There are over 800 Keys, so don't worry about overdoing it. Okay, see that last lonely piece of poppadum to your left? That's Key West.

(FYI: There are scores of other islands located *west* of Key West such as the angling-rich Marquesas and the historic Dry Tortugas with Fort Jefferson, but they are uninhabited -- if you don't count the odd whacko, eccentric, dirtbag or wannabe pirate).

Key West is about one mile by three miles, or two miles by four miles, depending how you measure or with whom you speak (small for an island, but big for a poppadum). It has in the neighbourhood of 28,000 inhabitants, more if you factor in any illegal aliens from the UK.

Over four million tourists visit Key West annually and the majority convey by automobile. If you rent a car at the airport in Miami, as we did, and drive down Highway #1 into the Keys you will have to cross 42 bridges including the adrenaline-rich Seven Mile Bridge to reach Key West. Highway #1 is also known as the Overseas Highway and it's the only road going in and the only road coming out. Many of the Keys are so narrow, you could throw a cricket ball into the Atlantic Ocean to your left or into the Gulf of Mexico to your right. Much of the 'highway' is only two lanes, so you can well imagine how lively it gets during hurricane season if authorities invoke a mandatory evacuation and the Overseas Highway becomes a 120-mile-long car park with thousands of panicked, hung-over tourists trying to escape an approaching tempestuous nightmare.

(FYI: In 1982, the crack U.S. Border Patrol set up a blockade in Florida City, the last stop on the mainland before reaching Key Largo. Their big plan was to block the never-ending flow of illicit drugs into 'America' from the unenforceable archipelago that is the Florida Keys.

If you were a resident of the Keys, but were by chance on the mainland, you had to wait in a patience-testing queue to suffer the indignity of showing your ID to get into the Keys and back home. This blockade created a horrendous bottle neck and a climate of annoyance for both locals and tourists. But the tourists -- bless their flexible little hearts -- only remained pissed-off for a short time, because then they just stopped coming.

Not good for a part of the world that is reliant on a crush of tourism -- and not good for Jimmy Buffett.

The mayor of Key West at the time was not amused by the Border Patrol treating the Florida Keys like a foreign country, so he and his cronies came up with a grand scheme: They would go to Federal Court in Miami and seek an injunction to stop the federal blockade. And they did just this, but things didn't go well 'up in America' and they were essentially laughed at. Not to be outdone by the big-city arrogance on the mainland, the mayor of Key West went to his backup plan and stepped out on to the courthouse steps and announced to the assembled TV crews, reporters and the world: 'Tomorrow at noon, the Florida Keys will secede from the Union!'

Well, you can imagine what a splash this made. In fact it provided the networks with something else to cover besides the latest congressional sex scandal.

The next day, at Mallory Square, the mayor of Key West read a proclamation of secession and proclaimed that Key West and the Florida Keys would now be known as the 'Conch Republic' and that it was an independent nation separate from the U.S. With no doubt the history books in mind -- and the coming election -- the mayor then symbolically began the Conch Republic's civil rebellion by breaking a loaf of stale Cuban bread over the head of a man dressed in a U.S. Navy uniform. After one minute of rebellion, the now 'Prime Minister' turned to the Admiral in charge of the Navy Base at Key West, surrendered to the 'Union Forces' and demanded one-billion dollars in foreign aid and war relief to rebuild the new nation -- the Conch Republic!

Mortified by the negative publicity, the intrepid U.S. Border Patrol immediately ceased and desisted. And to this day Key West and the Florida Keys still revel in the appellation of Conch Republic, and they have flags, hats, T-shirts, a fun spring/summer independence-day celebration, fairly authentic-looking passports and a nifty motto: 'We seceded where others failed.')

Since you've asked, I'll tell you that a 'conch' is someone who has been born in the Florida Keys; the name's derived from the coveted conch shell, a large spiral-shelled marine gastropod mollusc.

* * *

The morning after the Cuban MiG had scorched the island, Gabrielle and I met Popcorn Joe on the canopied upstairs back deck of the Pineapple Guest House for the infusion of caffeine -- and, yes, to find out how to apply for a Conch Republic passport. I'd purchased three Cuban con leches from the little market downstairs. And just so you know, a coffee con leche, if made the Cuban way, does wonders for a hangover.

We had a few sips of the Cuban coffee, then I said: 'If the offer still stands, we'd love to come and work for you.'

Popcorn Joe took another sip of his *con leche*, watched a frigate bird circle lazily overhead, then said: 'You both do have work permits, don't you?'

Long beat.

Dead silence.

'Ah, your faces are slaying me!' Popcorn Joe roared with laughter. 'Do I strike you as the kind of guy who obeys the law? Go take a look at your new home.'

There was a door off the back deck that led to the attic. We opened the door and saw a set of steep stairs leading up into thin air. Next to the stairs were a hot plate with two rings, and a drawer with two forks, two spoons and one knife.

'We have a kitchen!' Gabrielle said.

'We can put a kettle on!' I said.

We took a look at the set of stairs.

'Have you ever seen steps so steep?'

'Only in horror films.'

We crept up the flight of stairs using our hands on the upper steps. At the summit we found a large open window that looked out on to the tin roof of the wooden building next door (part of the Pineapple Guest House compound). To the right was an ugly desk, a small refrigerator that was more of a mini-bar, a ratty rattan table with an excuse-for-a-lamp and two wicker-less chairs. This was the living room. I switched on the lamp. A fifteen-watt bulb illuminated nothing.

We tried standing up straight, but could only do so where there was an open skylight. I peeped out the skylight and could see the masts of the schooners down at the seaport. With just my head sticking up above the tin roof, if anybody could see me, I would look like a man driving a tank. The skylight was left open, as was the window, to let the heat out. But not that much heat seemed to want out. It was hot enough to bake bread up here.

'Don't think we'll be doing much entertaining,' Gabrielle observed.

'Why?'

'Look.'

Behind me, in the middle of the living room, was the commode. It was completely exposed (as would the person 'riding the porcelain bus'). Next to the commode was a shower stall.

'The architect must have been on drugs,' Gabrielle said.

There was a glass partition with a door that separated the living room-cum-bog from the bedroom. We opened the door and ducked into our bedroom. The bedroom sported a double-bed, a small table and an old TV with an aluminium-foil antenna. We looked back at the commode.

'You'll be able to watch the TV from the throne,' I said.

'And that can be a good thing sometimes,' Gabrielle said.

'We are one lucky couple.'

'We'll work a little magic and turn this place into home-sweet-attic.'

The attic was the worst place that we had ever set eyes upon in our lives. There was no A/C. There were no ceiling fans. And we were beside ourselves with joy.

We went back downstairs, told Joe that the place was more than we could have ever hoped for, then we all sat there for a few moments watching a parrot flit about from palm tree to palm tree.

'You staying, means family from the UK will be coming here in droves,' Joe mused. 'They can stay in the efficiency when they do. No charge if they buy us lots of beer.' Then: 'You can move in upstairs today and start tomorrow if you want, but first take a look at this.' And on that he handed Gabrielle the Mullet Wrap.

I stood up and read over Gabrielle's shoulder, and the headlines made the hair on the back of my neck stand up: A Cuban Air Force major had defected with an appropriated MiG fighter. He had buzzed the island of Key West then landed at the nearby Naval Air Station. U.S. officials were in a quandary: Should the United States Navy be thrilled that it now had a Cuban MiG in its possession, or be deeply concerned that a world-class jet fighter from a hostile country had easily scooted beneath their not-so-state-of-the-art radar and landed wholly undetected in the very backyard of the Navy's premier pilot training facility for 'transient tactical aviation squadrons'. (And where the military population consists of 1,650 inescapably mortified active-duty; 2,507 hoping-for-a-transfer family members; 35 glad-it-didn't-happen-on-my-watch reservists; and 1,312 considering-a-career-change civilians).

'You should hop on your bicycles and take a ride out there,' Joe said. 'Tell me what you see. We'll meet for beers after Sunset Celebration tonight.'

This was too good to pass up, so Gabrielle and I finished our con leches, hopped on our bikes and rode out to the neighbouring key only to find out Boca Chica is NOT the neighbouring key, Stock Island is. We had to ride a whole lot farther to get to Boca Chica and then once there we took the old Boca Chica road. If you do this, and haven't expired from the effort, you can ride right along the Naval Air Station. Near the end of old Boca Chica Road the terrain narrows. The ocean is only about ten metres to your left. To your right, a mere five metres away, is a fence and the very end of the runway for the Naval Air Station. Exciting, but somehow disconcerting to be so close to the end of an active military runway.

The weather was glorious, so we hung around hoping to spot the MiG, but the humiliated powers-that-be already had it under wraps. If you make a flagrant cock-up one day, it's always best to cover your arse the next.

With nothing to see (and unaware that Key West's top nude beach was just past the Dead End sign), we decided to turn around and head back, but just as we were about to pedal away, something breached our attention. Way down at the far end of the runway were shimmering lights. A group of U.S. jet fighters was about to take off. This could be good crack, I thought, to be able to stand dead at the end of a runway when one of these high-powered machines took off and rocketed just overhead. Gabrielle concurred.

We heard a sound like distant thunder as one of the jet fighters began its roll-out. We watched as its image shimmered in the heat rising off the runway. The thunder increased in volume and the shimmering image grew larger and larger. Wow, were we ever the lucky ones. Here we were only a matter of a few feet from the end of the runway and the bloody jet was coming straight at us! Unfortunately, what no one had mentioned, and our dim brains could not grasp all on their own, was that these American fly-boys love it when they spy lonely sods like us straddling bicycles down at the end of their precious runway. The lead pilot and his supersonic F-14 Tomcat lifted off, then hugged the runway like a Hoover hugs that awful carpet in your auntie's lounge. When that banshee screamed right over our heads with a hellatious roar, we must have looked like the bloke who sticks his finger in the electrical outlet. All of our synapses were crackling at the same time and we thought the tops of our heads were going to blow off. Instead of rotating and climbing according to policy, the naval pilot tried to give us a Mohawk -- and he almost succeeded. Such noise! We thought the MiG had been low and noisy. Whereas the MiG shot over the beach at around a hundred feet, the American fighter cleared us by only twenty feet, and we felt the searing heat from his engines as bits of sand and coral sandblasted us from head to foot. He then rotated and shot skyward and 38-million-dollars worth of aircraft made a foamy wake in the shallow waters like the asteroid did in that movie.

I told the audiology god that if he would restore our hearing then we would never attempt something so foolish again -- ever.

(FYI: Enter **www.airnav.com/airport/NQX**, scroll down to the aerial photo and you can see this runway at the Naval Air Station coming straight at you, the sliver of a road and its proximity to the beach. If you look closely, you might be able to make out the precise location where two brain-dead bicyclists shit their shorts.)

* * *

**Author's Note: After eight months of secret planning, that Cuban Air Force major, who had defected to Boca Chica Naval Air Station in his MiG, flew back to Cuba in a borrowed Cessna 310.

The major may have known how to fly a sophisticated MiG, but he had to take lessons to learn how to handle the simplified twin-prop Cessna. The major departed from Marathon (50 miles up the Keys from Key West) and thoroughly familiar with the Cuban air defence system flew undetected under Cuban radar. Forty-five minutes later he slowed, banked over the translucent waters of northern Cuba and set his plane down on the narrow Varadero Highway between a truck and a bus. Our hero brought his Cessna to a sudden stop and out of the jungle his wife and two sons appeared. And then, with his precious cargo onboard, the major rolled out down the highway, lifted into the skies above Cuba, banked once and headed for Florida, freedom and a future.

CHAPTER 5

The next morning before we started our duties at the guest house we rendezvoused with Popcorn Joe for a *con leche* on his back deck. Sitting above a tropical garden getting wired on Cuban rocket fuel was a glorious way to start the day, and it evolved into a morning ritual.

The Pineapple Guest House was actually a compound comprised of three detached wooden houses -- divided into eight apartments -- a small swimming pool, coconut palms, travelling palms, bougainvillaea, cats and, as we were soon to discover, scorpions. The compound was located on the corner of Caroline Street and Peacon Lane and it was surrounded by Americana in the form of a white picket fence. Popcorn Joe had cut out the shapes of pineapples in the fence at ten-foot intervals to enhance the decor and mimic the gingerbread style of the island.

You may remember, from the Yellow Pages, the apartments rented by the night, week, month or season. Some guests stopped for just a few nights as they passed through the lower Keys, others came for the entire winter. There was no maid, so if you rented from Popcorn Joe, no one banged on your door or walked in on you when walking in just wasn't prudent.

When a gagging-for-it honeymoon couple, or family of twelve, or illegal number of college coeds checked out, Gabrielle and I would lay siege to the apartment and -- depending on how long you stayed, or how hard you partied -- restore it to life by cleaning, painting, repairing, airing and spraying. As you can imagine we were always a bit hesitant to enter an apartment after a long-term let. We always feared the worst. Having said that, the worst offenders were always the short-term groupies who followed the Offshore Powerboat Races. They always struck us as a twisted bunch and they held the record for irresponsibility. We found everything from an apartment that had obviously been used as a toilet (not the toilet used as a toilet, the *apartment*), to a cheese and sausage pizza between the sheets, to even a plateful of cocaine under the bed. We never asked our guests what they had been up to (and I never heard of anyone in Key West having cocaine leftover).

Other chores included vacuuming the pool, ridding the pool's filter of suntan lotion and harpooning the coconuts that fell out of the palm trees and into the pool. Hosing down the front sidewalk every morning, along with hosing down my bare feet, was my most cherished duty.

Gabrielle and I performed our glamorous menial chores for about three or four hours per day. Popcorn Joe paid us by the hour, our rent was free (as you know) and we were never going to get rich doing this -- and we were probably about as happy as a couple could be. Key West has a laid-back attitude and -- other than worrying about if your beer was going to get too warm -- stress was something that didn't seem to exist.

After the completion of our duties for the day, about noon or one in the afternoon, we would head over to Ft. Zack to swim, snorkel and lie prone. The attire in Key West is as you can imagine beyond casual, so we would bike to the beach wearing just our flippies and cossies. And soon we were as brown as those two Cuban boys we had seen fishing on the pier that very first day we had arrived.

* * *

Popcorn Joe found out that we were still renting our wheels, so he suggested we pay a visit to an industrious character out on Washington Street who restored and sold old bicycles. We took a glacially slow bus out there (we would have gotten there sooner had we walked) and found a leafy backyard that appeared to be a cloning clinic for used bikes. Curiously, all the bicycles were spray painted black.

'You can have anyone you want for fifty-dollars,' a retired felon told us. 'Take your pick. They've all been thoroughly gone over and everything and they're ready to ride.'

The first bike I tested would only turn to the left and it was very obvious that these bikes hadn't been 'gone over' by anybody, especially this funny old man, but we felt sorry for him so we kept riding around in circles until we found two good bikes that would go in a straight line.

And now we had jobs, a roof (literally the roof) over our heads and a mode of conveyance.

* * *

To celebrate our first 'hump day' at the guest house, Popcorn Joe invited us to an evening of abandon in the Old Town. He said he would drag along a few 'bent' residents from the Pineapple Guest House and we would drink until we ran out of money. What did he mean by 'bent'?

'The evening will give you good insight into the kind of folk that flee the real world and take refuge down here in Key West in the winter,' Joe informed us. 'It will be an eye-opener.'

An evening of testing beer in loud boisterous pubs with colourful characters of questionable mental health seemed the perfect way to pass time in paradise.

We convened our foray at our local, the Bull & Whistle, and it was here that Gabrielle and I met Roger, the former stockbroker from Seattle, and we also made the acquaintance of Bobbie Jo, the biker-chick from hell, I mean Alabama. Roger bore a striking resemblance to a certain shamed peer.

Bobbie Jo had the warmth of steak tartar and an *extremely* tight T-shirt which read: 'You Call Me Bitch Like That's a Bad Thing'. But she was pleasant enough once you found your way past the piercings and the bray-hams scented perfume that announced her arrival before she came into view.

We listened to a Country & Western singer up on stage sing the heartfelt lyrics: 'I'D RATHER BE HERE...DRINKIN' A BEER...THAN FREEZIN' MY ASS IN THE NORTH...'

And the conversation deteriorated from life on the treadmill to Harleys to dating. Popcorn Joe's idea of the perfect woman was blonde, big hooters and anywhere between the ages of eighteen and nineteen. Bobbie Jo said her perfect man didn't have to have lots of money if he could service motorcycles -- and her.

Everyone laughed.

'I'm serious!' Bobbie Jo whined.

Then Roger said that was his idea of the perfect man, as well.

Gabrielle and I exchanged looks.

We were at the Bull, 'just to warm up', so after a few drinks, we exited stage right and fell in with a passing herd of zebra.

Farther up Duval, we splintered from the herd (at a zebra crossing), slowed to a stroll and fought our way towards Jimmy Buffett's Margaritaville. Once again, the temperature was balmy and the street was filled with enough conflicting smells to take your olfaction on a spicy roller-coaster ride. On the way we spotted the usual suspects: Joke-Man working the crowd, the python wrangler draping his boa constrictor over the ba-zillionth tourist that day (one day that snake was going to have had enough with Show Business and squeeze the living you-know-what out of somebody) and Captain Jerry trolling for thirty-seven cents.

Just when you think you've run into all the weird creatures in God's world, someone surprises you. We were almost to Margaritaville when a Sidney Greenstreet type, all flabbily fat with bulbous pink cheeks and multiple chins, and dressed in all white, with a white Panama hat, sidled up to us and for no reason announced: 'I'm seventy-seven-years old and I have all my teeth.' He didn't want money. He wasn't inebriated or on drugs. He just wanted to let us know.

Margaritaville is a tourist-trap bar/restaurant, but a good one. The trappings included live music, a gift shop with good books on Key West and Parrot Head memorabilia (a Parrot Head is a rabid cult follower of Jimmy Buffett -- who is known for his island-escapist music), and a curious sign with this whimsically threatening warning: 'All shoplifters will be bound and gagged and forced to listen to a repertoire of Barry Manilow tunes.'

We took a table up by the band and had just settled in when someone suddenly tapped me on the shoulder. I swivelled round and actually physically jumped: It was Councillor George Redmond from back home in Glasgow. 'Oh, hiya, George,' I said meekly. 'What are you doin' here?'

'I came to check on youse, Jon and Gabrielle, youse said yer were going fer only a week!'

Oh, shit.

And then George burst out laughing. 'Great tae see youse, I'm just on my holidays. Enjoy yerself, see you when you get back.' And on that George took his leave.

'He's really tanned,' Gabrielle noted, then we ordered beers (and a shot of Tequila to calm my nerves) and we turned back to Popcorn Joe, Roger and Bobbi Jo -- as we knew it was destined to do -- the conversation dipped to a new low level as Bobbie Jo ventured into the arena of orgasms. Bobbie Jo could go all night long if she wasn't taking drugs. 'I had eight consecutive orgasms once,' Bobbie Jo informed us. 'I was trying for nine, but my partner died. Shoot. And he treated me like a lady.'

Everyone laughed.

'I'm serious!'

We heard a few more horror stories and had a few more beers, then Roger stood up and announced: 'Should've taken a pee two beers ago.'

I looked over at Gabrielle and she gave me a 'What planet are we on?' look back.

When Roger returned, we repaired to our next port-of-call, the Conch Seafood Farm (on the way, Bobbie Jo lit up a cigar). The Conch Seafood Farm is located right on the boardwalk at the Historic Seaport. We took seats at the bar. The bar is long. Seriously long. In fact, it's the longest bar between Miami and Havana for those of you keeping score. And the atmosphere here is decidedly end-of-the-world wharf.

A rascal up in a poorly lit corner was playing Jimmy Buffett songs (songs we had just heard at Margaritaville) and our bartender was good-natured and not at all sober. This is a good place to hang if you want the Key West charm without the neuroses of Duval.

Gabrielle drank a Mojito. Roger and Bobbie Jo drank Corona beers. Popcorn Joe and I drank Buds -- for a reason. Popcorn Joe had shown me a cartoon that morning. It was of a horse drinking out of a bucket labelled 'Coors' and simultaneously pissing into one marked 'Corona'.

The night went on and on, as alcohol-driven nights such as these tend to do, and it became hot and heavy and wall-to-wall sweaty bodies in the bar. And then someone rang a ship's bell to signal 'last call' and magically a truth of life was exposed as all the beauteously challenged women sitting at the bar suddenly had suitors (just like that line in that Country & Western song 'GIRLS GET PRETTIER AT LAST CALL').

And it was during the last-minute flesh frenzy that some profoundly pissed misguided city-slicker from New Orleans even found Bobbie Jo attractive. A real stretch.

Mr Big Easy sidled up to Sweet Home Alabama and drawled: 'How 'bout it, pretty baby, mind if I have the last dance?'

The music had stopped an hour earlier, but that didn't seem to deter these two as they only had eyes (and lust) for each other. As Mr Bourbon Street placed his hand on Bobbie Jo's butt and steered her out on to a dance floor that wasn't there, we heard Bobbie Jo coo: 'Well, shoot, sugar, I do believe God put me on this earth as a gift to you...'

Gabrielle and I shot Popcorn Joe a look and he whispered back: 'Winter can be weird down here.'

CHAPTER 6

After work one day, Gabrielle and I decided to venture deeper into the Old Town and explore more of the island. Gentle trade winds were blowing as we hopped on our bikes and rode two blocks over to Duval, then turned right and pedalled down in the direction of the glass-bottom boat. Just before we reached the harbour, we swung left on Front Street and headed one block over to Whitehead Street. Our plan was to ride our bikes under the canopy of shade trees along Whitehead Street and down to the highly acclaimed Southernmost Point -- the most southerly part of the continental United States.

But wait! Before we get going, what's that? No, that! That behemoth, terracotta brick building over there. Let me just consult the guidebook I have jammed in the back pocket of my Jams. Oh, so that's what it is. This was once the old Customs House, but now it's the Museum of Art & History. And here's one for you: The Customs House was built with a steeply slanting roof -- as were all government buildings built in America at that time (circa 1890). They were built in this dramatic fashion so the snow would slide off when it became too deep. Located at 24 degrees north latitude, the island of Key West is situated within the subtropical region of the western hemisphere. On account of its proximity to the Gulf Stream and the Gulf of Mexico, Key West's average summer and winter temperatures rarely differ more than 5 degrees Celsius. In the deepest, darkest depths of winter, Key West has never reported frost, ice, sleet -- and certainly never snow.

The January average high is 22C, the average low 19C.

Paradise, indeed.

We left the snow-ready roof of the old Customs House behind in our wake and slowly pedalled past the Mel Fisher Museum (shipwrecked treasure, alas, costs a fortune to get in) and the Audubon House (enjoy the tropical gardens and fine works of John James Audubon, celebrated ornithologist) and came upon Kelly's Restaurant on the corner of Whitehead and Caroline. Kelly's is owned by the actress Kelly McGillis (*Top Gun*), and the building was the original home to Pan American World Airways. Apparently it's important to replace one fading icon with another.

We carried on past the Post Office, the point where Highway #1 ends at Mile Marker zero, and came to the corner of Southard and Whitehead. Here on the left corner is a watering hole popular with the locals. It's called the Green Parrot and it has a killer slogan -- albeit stolen from the novelist W Somerset Maugham's description of Monaco in the 1920s -- 'A Sunny Place for Shady People'.

The Green Parrot (a Key West landmark since 1890) is the first and last bar on U.S. Highway #1, and a sign tells us it's the 'HOME OF GREAT DRINKS AND BAD ART, POOL, DARTS AND PINBALL'. This place can rock in the fragrant heat late at night and when it does it gets chocka. (Later, we would see locals with folding chairs or lawn chairs they'd brought from home sitting outside on the sidewalk, swilling pints, soaking up the sounds and endeavouring to keep cool.)

Keep pedalling! Now off to our right and down Petronia Street is Bahama Village. Bahama Village is where Bahamian, Haitian and Cuban immigrants settled when they first came to Key West in the 1800s. It's an ethnic section of ramshackle tin-roofed houses, island-cuisine restaurants, funky Caribbean cafés, wild roosters, rusted out cars, drug dealers and, by night, danger. If Key West has a ghetto, this is it. Having said that, it also has charm -- lots of it. Would it surprise you to learn that the area is being gentrified as rich folk from up North slowly buy up the ramshackle old houses from the low-income families? Sadly, many of Key West's original denizens can no longer afford the skyrocketing property taxes and have had to move out of the very house they were born in. More on this front anon.

Our shirts are sticking to our backs as we carry on down Whitehead Street, pedal a bit farther and come to the corner of Olivia and Whitehead. Perhaps we shouldn't have attempted this tour in the heat of the day, shade trees or not. But wait! Yes, wait again! What's that over there, just off to our left and hidden behind that crumbling brick wall? No, not that way. That way. Why it's none other than the Ernest Hemingway Home and Museum. If Key West is the world headquarters for cats, which it just may well be, then Hemingway's very house is the world headquarters for six-toed cats. That's right -- cats with six toes. Museum docents knowingly tell perspiring tourists that Hemingway brought the first 'polydactyl' cat over from Cuba and the descendants (of the cats) roam the island today. But the truth is that Hemingway didn't have cats when he lived in the house. He adored cats but his wife at the time, Pauline, was just a titch ailurophobic (I had to look it up) and wanted peacocks -- so peacocks it was. Hemingway did however have cats -- lots of them -- when he lived in San Francisco de Paula, Cuba -- after he dumped Pauline (and the peacocks).

(FYI: Nowadays, the Hemingway House and Museum is home to, get ready, sixty cats. About half of the cats at the museum are polydactyl, with those extra furry toes. When you see these little critters slinking about, it appears as if they are wearing après-ski boots.)

When Hemingway wasn't deep-sea fishing, or drinking all of Sloppy Joe's rum, he was writing. Somehow, back-then, backwater Key West stimulated Hemingway, and it was here he worked on many of his great works: *Death in the Afternoon*, *Green Hills of Africa*, *To Have and Have Not*, *The Snows of Kilimanjaro* and *For Whom the Bell Tolls* -- at least that's what the folk at the museum say (according to Patrick Hemingway, Hemingway's son, some of the best fiction coming out of Key West is what the guides at the museum say transpired when Ernest was in situ).

Across the street from the Hemingway House is the Key West lighthouse. The hyperbole du jour is that Hemingway purchased this particular house as it was across the street from the lighthouse and he wanted to be able to find his way home after a night of drinking at Sloppy Joe's.

And couldn't we all use a lighthouse from time to time?

We continued our journey past the lighthouse and soon came to the local chapter of Alcoholics Anonymous, affectionately known as 'Anchors Aweigh'. Here we found a group of end-of-the-line, mangy curs loitering out front in the shade of a palm tree -- and these were just the women: shaken, lost souls who all looked as if they could use a really stiff drink.

Not wanting to stir any dissension in the ranks with my T-shirt, which read: 'ONE TEQUILA...TWO TEQUILA...THREE TEQUILA...FLOOR!', Gabrielle and I sped farther down Whitehead.

And then, right there before us was the sparkling Atlantic Ocean. It had only taken us a couple pages in this book to pedal right across the island. Imagine.

Smack on the edge of the lapping waves was the frighteningly large, red, black and yellow buoy marking the Southernmost Point and '90 miles to Cuba'. Tourists were swarming all around this nine-foot monolith, happily snapping away with throwaway cameras, and I didn't have the heart to tell them that this really wasn't the true

Southernmost point in the continental United States. That distinction belongs to a little blob of land a few blocks to our right, which just happens to be on Navy property and thus strictly *prohibido* -- unless, of course, you are defecting from Cuba.

(FYI: The true southernmost point in the entire United States is actually on the Big Island of Hawaii, in Ka Lae, for those of you taking notes, where the next landfall by the way is a mere 7500 miles away. When Hawaii became the 50th state in 1959, Key West had to add the continental disclaimer. Riveting.)

We biked one block back to Duval Street to a clean well-lighted bookshop called L. Valladares & Son, located at 1200 Duval Street. This is the oldest newsstand in Key West, and the best. It's a place where Hemingway had a line of credit (even though it wasn't a bar), and it offers a huge selection of national and regional newspapers, magazines, literary journals, paperbacks and old postcards.

We went inside and had a little snoop around. This is a place where you could clearly spend some time. So we spent some time. Eventually we found the book we were looking for, so we worked our way back to the till through Gay Fiction. At the till we found a cat (traditional five-toed, thank you very much) snoozing on top of a stack of the *New York Times*. Sometimes that newspaper puts me to sleep, as well. We paid for the book and then I consulted my watch. We still had time to make it to the beach if we hurried.

* * *

Gabrielle and I skidded to a halt, dismounted and leaned our bicycles against a palm tree at the beach at Ft. Zack. We first looked towards the breakwater, then over by the concession stand. Finally, we scanned the waves. A tanned swimmer was cleaving the surf in a jerky fashion made so by handmade fins.

Shark-Man saw us, waved and came ashore.

'Here,' Gabrielle said, handing him the paperback we had just purchased at the bookshop.

Shark-Man eyed the book and a big smile swept across his face: '*Notes from a Small Island*!' he said. 'For me?'

'For you.'

'Hey, hang on. I've got something I want to give you, too.'

Shark-Man reached into the pocket of his cossie and pulled out a small, colourful seashell. It's a "cat's-eye",' he said. 'It brings good luck. I always make sure I have one like this with me whenever I go in the ocean. I found it right out there.'

Gabrielle took the cat's-eye and we thanked Shark-Man and then we pedalled off to Mallory Square to catch sunset.

And later that night we saw Shark-Man sitting at a café on Duval Street, sipping a beer and reading his book.

And to this day, whenever we travel, Gabrielle and I always carry that cat's-eye with us for good luck.

* * *

Key West is a literary town. And at all levels of society. If you pop your head into the library, you will find most of the island's homeless in there reading books, perusing the newspapers and pouring through magazines. The fact that it's a sticky 80 degrees outside and the library is air-conditioned and cold enough to hang meat inside may have something to do with it, but what the heck. In Key West, it's not uncommon to see transients sitting on park benches, passing the day at the beach under swaying palms or lazying in the shade under sprawling banyan trees, reading.

Key Westers have always loved to improve their brains.

In the mid-19th century, the cigar industry transformed Key West into the thirteenth largest port in the country. To get an education, and to relax while they worked, the cigar-makers hired lectors to read books and newspapers out loud. These lectors read in both English and Spanish. In the morning, one lector would read Cuban newspapers. In the afternoon, another lector would read from Alexander Dumas, Blasco Ibanez, Eduardo Zamacois -- even Shakespeare.

Key West, a literary town, with a captive audience, at all levels.

CHAPTER 7

As winter turned to spring, the cold fronts stopped marching through, birdsong heralded the mild mornings, an explosion of floral colour echoed about the island and, mercifully, the snowbirds packed up their egos, jumped into their defile-the-environment SUVs and polluted their way back up North.

High season was finally winding down and with the long-awaited migration of the wannabe Key Westers a pleasant transformation took place: Key West was returned to the locals and the pace of life slowed to that of years gone by.

And our duties at the guest house slowed to a trickle.

With a diminished workload, Gabrielle and I were able to complete our chores midmorning and then we would hop on our bikes and explore Key West's narrow tropical lanes before it became too hot and we would be forced to make tracks for the beach. And it was while we were peregrinating the back tropical lanes that we started to become familiar with Key West's glorious floral wonders.

One such delight was the Royal Poinciana. A Royal Poinciana in bloom is a devastatingly beautiful sight, you see, this is a flowering tree with five-inch flowers and the colours may vary from crimson to scarlet to orange to salmon. There are even trees streaked with yellow or white. It's an eye-popping moment when you round a corner on your bicycle and behold a Royal Poinciana for the first time. Imagine seeing a tree sixty-feet tall that appears as scorching red as a Key West sunset.

As we tooled about the back lanes, dodging falling coconuts, screeching feral cats and a frightful number of wild chickens, we would come upon little bursts of colour in the form of plumeria and gardenia and hibiscus and bird-of-paradise, and then if we pedalled about at night, which we often did since our attic was holding at ninety degrees till after midnight, we would discover night-blooming jasmine and even gigantic blooming cacti. And it was never difficult to find these night-blooming joys, for the moment we entered a darkened lane somewhere, the rich sweet scent of the blossoms would lead us like a cartoon character down the alley and right to the very source.

* * *

Early one spring morning we were sitting under the canopy out on the back deck with Popcorn Joe sipping our traditional kick-your-arse Cuban coffee. Classical music was seeping out of the cottage across the back lane, a couple of wild chickens were pecking at the ground and a tropical shower was giving the island a good watering. It may have been raining, but we could still see blue sky and large billowy clouds off to the south. Soon a rainbow formed and we all stared in silent wonder at its deep, rich colours. The moisture from the shower enhanced the heady fragrances of frangipani and honeysuckle and all three of us sat there in a tranquil, giddy stupor, not unlike a cat that has been given catnip. I looked over at my wife and she just smiled dreamily back, and I knew what she was thinking. We liked Key West -- we liked Key West a lot.

Eventually, Popcorn Joe broke the reverie with: 'The slow weeks at the guest house are going to continue until the Spring Breakers pillage the island. I'm going to have to cut your hours even more.'

Gabrielle and I went pale.

'Ah! You should see your faces! I've got a great scheme for you. Why don't you guys think up some sort of craft to sell down at Mallory. I know everybody on the board, so there shouldn't be any trouble getting you juried.'

Popcorn Joe went on to tell us that the evening Mallory migration had started back in the '60s when local hippies, day-tripping on LSD, used to go down to Mallory every evening to 'watch Atlantis rise mythically out of the cloud formations at sunset'. Then in the late '70s and '80s, when Mallory became a popular venue for tourists, fledgling entrepreneurs began showing up at sunset to flog their wares -- both legitimate and otherwise -- and a flea market-cum-head shop was born. Needless to say the nearby purported legitimate merchants, who had their custom siphoned off every sunset, were not amused by the 'morally contaminated' competition down at Mallory Docks, so they made waves -- big waves -- not good on an island that is only 18 feet above sea level at its highest point.

The local merchants were backed by big bucks and the ineffable power of City Hall, but they clearly underestimated their adversary -- the little people.

Rule #1 in Key West: NEVER FUCK WITH THE LITTLE PEOPLE.

Led by tightrope walker Will Soto, the little people formed a nonprofit organization called the Key West Cultural Preservation Society -- and as we all know there's nothing that will make your blood run colder than a nonprofit organization.

To the ire of the mainstream, Main Street vendors, the Cultural Preservation Society 'kicked some legal butt' and leased Mallory Docks during the sunset hours.

Gabrielle and I were keenly interested, so we asked Popcorn Joe what we had to do to break in.

'You have to create the craft or artwork yourself,' Popcorn Joe began. 'And you have to have at least three steps in the crafting process to go through to prove to the jury that you've indeed 'created' it. Keeps the unscrupulous riffraff from importing kitsch from the Third World and flogging it down on the pier.'

That evening Gabrielle and I went down to Sunset early and observed the Hat Man as he wove his palm fronds into hats and bowls. And we talked to Claudia Richards and a fellow named 'Buschi' about hand-painting designs on T-shirts, and Jewelry Joanne and Jewelry Annie enlightened us to their world of handmade jewellery, and we were also given the low-down from Deirdre about sculpting roses and geckoes and mangroves out of copper. Deirdre told us to 'feel closer to her art, she would sculpt in the nude'. Gabrielle noted that many of Deirdre's masterpieces needed to be welded, so of course we wondered if she wore the goggles.

Besides the craft vendors, there were also those caricature artists and food vendors and tarot card readers and escape artists and various other performers that I told you about in the opening chapters. There certainly were a lot of possibilities, in fact, there were so many, Gabrielle and I soon realised that we had absolutely no talent or skills in any of these arenas.

But then one day everything changed.

We were walking down Duval Street. A cruise ship was in and we were doing our best to avoid the upper-crust as they flitted from shop to shop defoliating the island like locusts -- loud, nautically dressed locusts. 'Oh, Harry look. Aren't those just the cutest little emerald earrings. I just have to have them. All of them...' Or, 'Gimme a break, Alice, what do you think I am, a walking ATM machine?...' Or, 'Remember, Ethyl, we only have three hours here, so let's buy as much authentic native art as we can so we can prove to the folk back home that we were really in the Caribbean...' Gag me.

Anyway, Gabrielle and I sought refuge in the Bull & Whistle and had a coffee, then when the locusts scurried back to their ship (lest they miss a free meal), we slipped across the street and stopped in front of Porter House where a series of small open-air galleries was set beneath a sprawling banyan tree. The banyan tree's branches and aerial roots were so vast and thick, they served as a canopy to the galleries below and kept out most of the rain -- usually.

Our purpose here in 'the garden' was industrial espionage. We hoped that we would be inspired by the artwork on display in these little outdoor establishments. One gallery stood out from the rest, and the artist who did all the paintings was actually there painting -- and not sitting in a bar somewhere -- so we spoke with him a bit. This fellow's name was Alberto. Alberto was an Italian artist from Rimini and he painted acrylics and watercolours of Key West's most popular sights such as: Sloppy Joe's Bar, the Audubon House, the Key West Lighthouse, the Hemingway House and the Porter House with a big banyan tree out front.

Alberto also had a painting depicting the setting sun and the performers down at the Sunset Celebration at Mallory Square.

'Sun, same sun everywhere,' Alberto told us. When Alberto spoke, he employed a maximum of gestures and a minimum of verbs. 'Here, Key West Chamber of Commerce market sunset and now sunset most famous in world.'

'Who deems it the most famous in the world?' Gabrielle asked.

'Key West Chamber of Commerce.'

I asked Alberto if he sold a lot of paintings with the Key West sunset in them.

'*Tutti giorni*,' Alberto gestured. 'Especially just after famous sunset.'

Alberto had a late-returning cruise-ship passenger, who made traditional neuroses seems like a good thing, so Gabrielle and I scarpered and sat in the warm sun upstairs on the balcony of the Bull & Whistle.

I ordered two piña coladas and then turned to Gabrielle: 'Are you thinking what I'm thinking?'

'Sunsets,' is all she had to say.

Our drinks came and we sat there for a while, sipping the coconut-pineapple beverages and tingling from our realisation -- or perhaps that was the rum. Then we blew out of the Bull and did a whirlwind tour of the town.

And our suspicions were proven correct.

'Everyone is painting the famous sunsets,' Gabrielle said, 'but no one is photographing the sunset. Let's sell them at the Sunset Celebration.'

Then Gabrielle gestured like Alberto: 'Famous sunset!'

'You are such a brain,' I said. 'I can't believe no one has ever thought of it.'

* * *

My father had been a professional photographer and I had grown up around cameras, f-stops, ASAs, telephoto lenses, filters, a darkroom and vats of vile smelling chemicals. And with this knowledge-rich background came a certain pedigree, I was about to join the legions of other progeny of successful creatives who knew absolutely fuck all about their professional parent's line of work.

Gabrielle and I had unearthed a niche, we just didn't have a clue how to go about exploiting it.

The next day we hopped on our bikes and pedalled out past the cemetery, through a leafy section of Key West known as the Meadows and emerged on North Roosevelt Boulevard. Here we paused, sat by the water, admired the houseboats and soaked up the sun. We could hear Cuban music coming from one of the houseboats. Havana Top 40.

A small group of pelicans soared lazily into view and we watched as they climbed, banked, stalled, then folded like an accordion and plunged -- feathery brown arrows shooting into the glassy water below.

Eventually we said good-bye to the pelicans and biked on past the Blue Lagoon Hotel (where the night clerk had been murdered the year before), the Jet-Ski rentals, and all the way to the Searstown strip mall where a good pawnshop was located. There are a handful of pawnshops on the island and a treasure trove of photographic equipment can be found amongst guns, golf clubs, used diving equipment, nameless junk and dead people's jewellery.

We leaned our bikes against a palm tree and entered the cool confines of the pawnshop. A sign on the front door read: ALL OFFERS CONSIDERED -- SOME FOR LONGER THAN OTHERS.

One thing I will tell you right up front, if you are ever in Key West and in the hunt for photographic equipment, this is the place to be. Nikon and Minolta and Canon and Olympus and Pentax and Leica and Big Bertha, the shop had them all. After thorough exploration, and much confusion, we found a 10-year-old Nikon with a 50 mm lens, a 200 mm telephoto and a 3X extension so we could triple the telephoto's effectiveness and sear our retinas. The equipment was reasonably priced and all very impressive and neither of us even knew how to load the camera.

We noticed a fellow wearing a motorcycle helmet rooting around in the camera section. Who keeps their motorcycle helmet on inside a shop? Okay, those guys, but who else? At first we thought he was there to knock over the pawnshop, but then we recognised him. His name was 'Wino' and he sold handmade jewellery down at the Sunset Celebration.

We told Wino about our intentions and he had a really good laugh. When he was finished laughing, braying actually, and obviously at our expense, he said these words: 'Oh, lots of people have thought of that idea. Nobody's ever been able to pull it off though.'

Oh, fuck. 'Why not?' I asked.

'Most of the photographers were crap, having studied at the Auto Trader school of photography.' Then: 'Have you ever tried shooting directly into a nuclear reaction? Weren't you always told to keep the sun at your back? You don't know nothin' do ya?'

Not to use double negatives, I thought.

We watched Wino leave the store, jump on his motorcycle and, still laughing, zoom off. Then Gabrielle and I paid for our camera equipment with our hard-earned money, loaded it all into my backpack and stepped out into the glaring nuclear sun. We squinted at the sky. Our eyes watered beyond belief. Then we climbed on our bicycles and pedalled through the white heat the long way back home.

* * *

For the next three weeks, every single night, Gabrielle and I headed down to Mallory and photographed the setting sun. Sometimes we shot 36 exposures, sometimes 72, sometimes more -- each night. Then, if we weren't too blind to find it, we would run around the corner to Pro Photo and have the photos developed. A young guy by the name of Scott took a liking to us and would do our photos within an hour, but not charge us the 'One Hour' rate. Then Gabrielle and I would speed home on our bicycles, sequester ourselves in our attic flat and pour over the photos. And guess what? Each and every shot of the setting sun was unmitigated crap. Key West was known for the most glorious sunsets on the planet, and through hard work and lack of talent, we had found a way to undo all the effort the Key West Chamber of Commerce had done over the previous years

We were in serious trouble.

Then one day, it dawned on Gabrielle what we had been doing wrong. We had risen early to watch the sunrise on the other side of the island. We watched the morning sky metamorphose from pitch black to one smeared with grey and then warm ribbons of phantasmagorical colour and then, the split second the sun was about to burst upon the horizon, Gabrielle yelled: 'I got it! Seeing it this way round all makes sense. We're shooting our sunsets when the sun is too high in the sky. The brightness is washing everything out. We have to shoot just as the sun is plopping on the horizon. The light will be florid and dramatic.'

I stared at Gabrielle and suddenly it all made sense. I had married one smart lass.

* * *

That evening, eager to test out Gabrielle's theory, we positioned ourselves up on the Havana Docks deck of the Pier House Resort. The Havana Docks is an outdoor bar, one storey above the water, and it's a great place to go to worship the sunset, listen to some island music and get hammered.

We set up our camera equipment along the white wooden railing that keeps drunks from falling into the harbour below, and waited. Shooting the sunset, we were slowly realising, was not unlike wildlife photography. You did *nada* for the longest time then all hell broke loose for a fleeting moment when the subject decided to make a run for it.

We heard the blast of a marine horn and turned to our left just in time to see the glass-bottom boat exit the harbour and set off on its Sunset Cruise. Then Gabrielle scooted off and ordered us drinks so the evening wouldn't be a total loss.

When Gabrielle returned we sipped tall tropical mystery drinks with little umbrellas and enjoyed the warm sun. We breathed in the inimitable island smells of saltwater, gardenias, suntan lotion and diesel fuel. There certainly were worse places to be and worse things to be doing. So what if we didn't capture a sunset with our camera tonight, we would at the least capture it with our eyes.

On a lark, Gabrielle picked up a copy of the Mullet Wrap and held it up in front of her (as hostages do) and asked me to take a photo. We were going to send it back to her mum in the UK. Her mum would be able to tell from the date on the newspaper precisely when the photo was taken, and that we were having glorious weather.

The sun sank lower and lower in the sky. The evening was setting up nicely. There were no clouds on the horizon to block the sun, but there was a canopy of high cirrus forming overhead that should light up once the colours of the setting sun began to explode.

We waited and waited and watched in awe as the sun grew in size. What was once a small searing fireball overhead, was transforming into the biggest glowing pumpkin you could ever imagine as it neared the Gulf of Mexico. Then, just at the moment the sun was about to kiss the horizon, we reeled off a fairly impressive series of shots and burned 36 exposures in just over two minutes as the sun squatted on the ocean and slipped over the backside of Mother Earth. We were drained, but exhilarated at the same time and it was all we could to do to remain upright as a flaming sky of rich magentas and deep purples lit up like the backdrop on a West End musical.

Mother Nature had given us what we wanted.

And everyone applauded.

We quickly packed up our gear, threw it all in my backpack, and rushed over to Scott at Pro Photo. Scott dutifully developed our roll of Kodak Gold 100 and then turned to us: 'I don't know how to tell you this, but I think you gave me the wrong roll.'

What? We couldn't believe our ears. 'What do mean?' I asked, shooting a look at Gabrielle.

'This can't be your roll,' Scott said, cracking a smile. 'This is damn good work.'

Too excited to pedal home, Gabrielle and I wended our way up Duval to the Bull & Whistle. We sat outside on the balcony overlooking the street below and poured over our prints. We were sitting in Key West at the end of March in shorts and T-shirts. It was tropical and balmy and you could smell the night-blooming jasmine. And out of 36 shots we had taken, we had six that we could sell to the tourists (and one where a sloshed local, hanging over a white wooden railing, was giving us the finger). We were ecstatic. Now all we had to do was pass the jurying process and we could set up on the pier at Mallory Square. It was quite the night to celebrate. And celebrate we did, indeed.

* * *

The next jurying for the Sunset Celebration wasn't until the following Wednesday, so we continued to burn roll after roll of film in our never-ending quest to catch the perfect Key West sunset. We were slowly learning the technique, but quickly realising that Mother Nature was calling the shots. If we could now return home with one good commercial shot out of 36 exposures, we were delighted.

When Wednesday arrived, we were late leaving to be juried. Here's what happened: We were just running out the front door, tripping over all our gear, when we heard a bloodcurdling racket emanating from the swimming pool out back of the guest house. It was a screaming-bloody-murder sound the likes of which I had only heard twice before in my life: Once on the Discovery Channel when a pride of lions was bent on savaging some poor little springbok, and once at the dentist during what had started out as a routine root canal. Gabrielle and I ran down the backstairs and found, get ready, a big fat rat caught in the pool's skimmer. The rat and the skimmer had conflicting agendas. The rat was fighting to stay above the surface and the skimmer was trying to suck him down.

I tried to snare the screeching, yellow-toothed creature with a pool net, but the head of the net wouldn't fit into the skimmer slot. Never a piker when it comes to creatures in need, I quickly slipped into Gabrielle's gardening gloves and, feeling and looking not at all macho, reached into the skimmer and plucked the bedraggled rodent by its twitching tail. Wild animals never understand that we are there to help and presumably after taking one look at me, the little pest began to screech even louder. Undeterred by the response, and only taking it just a bit personally, I transported the beleaguered beast across the back alley and released him under the cottage where some snooty folk from West Palm Beach had a second home.

We then hopped on our bikes and pedalled like the wind over to an old school building near the library. It was here that we were to be juried. We were nervous as cats, but we knew we had Popcorn Joe there in our corner to guide us through the process.

We slunk into a stuffy, sweaty classroom and saw four other candidates who hoped to be juried by the four jurors present. Everyone turned and glared at us.

'You're late!' came a sharp voice.

'Sorry,' I said. 'Rat in the skimmer.' And we were the recipients of the most withering of looks.

We sat down in the dead middle of a hostile atmosphere and I whispered to Gabrielle: 'Who are these people doing the jurying? I've never seen any of them before in my life. I thought we knew everybody down at Mallory.'

We watched anxiously as the various hopefuls did their demonstration and were ripped limb from limb, eviscerated and eaten alive. The carnivorous jurors were enjoying their power.

Each shaky-kneed candidate had to demonstrate the critical three steps. A dizzy young lady in a tank top, who wanted to sell handmade jewellery, had to cut the shape out of some precious metal (like tin), step one, then glue kitschy plastic sparkly crap to an ill-advised shape, step two, and then attach a hook, step three, so it all would form a monumentally ugly earring in anyone's social circle.

The next great artisan was some older bloke in a tie-dye top and silver ponytail. This aging love-child looked as if he had gone through the Sixties twice. With quivering hands he demonstrated to the jury, in three steps, how to make different types of pipes: coffin pipes and bud bombs and fimo pipes. Then he assured the jury that the pipes would only be sold for the smoking of tobacco and nothing more sinister. After all, this was Key West, and who would ever doubt a dude in tie-dye.

The jurors gave him a look of 'Are you fucking shitting me!' and he was in, in like flint.

The other two nervous wrecks fumbled their way through the jurying process: a handsome bloke making sandals with real fruit on them and a German woman whose quest in life was to sell tie-dye baby clothes. Presumably she had done her market research and there was a big call for that sort of thing.

They both passed and were accepted on the pier.

Then it was our turn. We showed the jury (who all seemed exceedingly uptight for folk living in paradise) our Nikon, the telephoto lens, the 3X extension, all of our lousy photos and then our killer prints. And do you know what one bloke said?

'So where's the three steps?'

I glanced over at Gabrielle and whispered: 'Do you see Popcorn Joe anywhere?'

Gabrielle just shook her head, then spoke directly and confidently to the jurors: 'We take the photos, then we mat the photos, then we hand-paint the frames and stick it all together.'

But one juror, a wet-lipped fleshy creature (who we would later learn rode around the island on a moped with flat tires looking for young boys) said: 'But do you do your own developing?'

I shot a look at Gabrielle and she whispered: 'Where's Popcorn Joe?'

Then, believe it or not, I remembered something my father had taught me as a kid. Yes, a light bulb had flickered on just like that time I switched it on by mistake in the darkroom: 'Can't do our own developing. Damn well won't do our own developing. And do you know why? I'll tell you why. As you know, there's a water shortage in the Florida Keys right now and developing colour uses a prohibitive amount of water.' Then, for justifiably desperate effect, I added: 'We work closely with Scott down at Pro Photo.'

The jury members looked at each other and all mumbled in unison and nodded their heads in solemn agreement. Then the first one said: 'Sounds good to me.' And the second one said: 'Yeah, me, too.' And the third one said: 'Yeah, let's let them on the pier.'

Everyone turned to the fourth juror, *el gordo* with the flat tires, the turd who made Truman Capote look butch, a man who made Simon Cowell seem soft and cuddly, and he scoffed: 'How do we know that you've taken the photos yourselves?'

I positively ached to strangle this bozo or worse jam a certain fleshy appendage of his in the pool skimmer -- not that it would have fit, mind you.

We were dead. There was no way we could prove we had shot this sunset ourselves. Even Scott down at Pro Photo had wondered who had really taken the photos.

And right about now, right when the tide was on its way out -- and fast -- my wonderful wife, who was always the coolest of cucumbers in the most distressing of situations, threw a photo down on to the table in front of the jurors. And the photo was of her holding up the Mullet Wrap, complete with visible date, and what sealed the deal for us was that the sun setting in the background was indisputably the same sun as the one in the six killer photos the jurors had just approved.

CHAPTER 8

The town is in a frenzy.

Bales of marijuana have washed up on the beaches on the Atlantic side of the island, and aging burnt-out hippies are hopping on their bicycles and racing to the shores.

Do you even believe this?

This is not a common occurrence in Key West -- nor is it a rare one. Fishing trawlers, shrimp boats and sexy 'cigarette' speedboats, laden with contraband, endeavour to reach an unofficial port of entry in the Florida Keys from Mexico, Central America and a Caribbean island of your choice. Profits are high and risks are low, for when the drug smugglers approach coastal waters they simply transfer the contraband to small 'go fast' water craft such as Jet-Skis, Ski-Doos and Zodiacs. The low radar signature of these zippy vessels makes it a daunting challenge at best for interdiction forces, and if the smugglers are spotted by roving Coast Guard cutters, the *contrabandistas* dump their booty into the sea and that's why it occasionally washes up on the beaches of the Lower Keys.

We were surprised to learn of the bales of weed washing up, and we were shocked when we heard that fishing boats were returning to port with packets of cocaine jammed down the gullets of big game fish. But neither of these prepared us for what we were to hear next. A young boy had died while on holiday with his family in Puerto Rico. When the grieving family returned to Miami with the body, an alert customs agent noticed baggage handlers struggling mightily with the boy's small wooden casket. How could that be? The customs agent ordered the body removed -- and weighed. The small child weighed fifty pounds more than he should have. The dead child's body had been cut open, nearly 25 kilos of cocaine had been secreted inside, and then the corpse had been sewn back up.

Okay, stay with me now.

Smugglers rented single-engine aircraft from various airports in and around Broward County (Ft. Lauderdale) and Dade County (Miami), then flew to nearby Caribbean islands (often Haiti or the Bahamas) to pick up contraband. The smugglers waited until nightfall then took off and headed back towards South Florida. Customs surveillance aircraft, operating in the hotbed of drug trafficking that is the Western Caribbean, spotted the private planes and followed from a distance as the aircraft entered American airspace. With sophisticated night vision scopes, custom agents could easily tail the smugglers until they decided to set down on some off-the-beaten-track dirt airstrip in the boondocks of South Florida.

But none of the single-engine aircraft ever landed in South Florida -- they all crashed. And it took government agents a long time to unravel the mystery of the downed aircraft. Law may have a 'long arm', but crime is always one step ahead and often out of reach. How did the smugglers do it? They eluded capture by putting the single-engine aircraft on auto-pilot, then they bailed out over the Everglades with the contraband strapped to their bodies. With airboats waiting for the parachutists at prearranged locations, escape was swift and exact. Meanwhile, the customs planes followed the offending (and now unmanned) aircraft for a hundred miles or more before the rented aircraft ran out of fuel, fell out of the sky and crashed.

So how did government agents crack this creative method of smuggling? They didn't, one of the pilots solved it for them, you see, a pilot/parachutist was found hanging in a hammock tree in the Everglades. He had 50 kilos of cocaine strapped to his body -- and a broken neck.

Besides the smuggling of illicit drugs, there's also the smuggling of Homo Sapiens. Cubans to be exact. This next bit is not publicised, but if you are a Cuban and you are no longer enamoured with the ideology of Fidel (or now his brother), and you want out, you can contact a relative in Miami through the Little Havana grapevine, who will contact a relative or friend in Key West, who will then pay a visit to one of a handful of speedboat skippers. These daring blokes will slip over to Cuba under cloak of darkness and pluck you and your family off a deserted Cuban beach, but the 'charter' is going to cost you -- often as much as ten-thousand dollars per person.

One local captain, in the spirit of *carpe p.m.*, made the crossing to Cuba one dark night, and just as he pulled up to a designated deserted beach not far from Havana, a Cuban gunboat burst out of nowhere and opened fire. The captain was hit in both legs. At last report, he's enriching his Spanish in a Cuban prison cell without the luxury of air conditioning.

Such horror stories abound, but so does the odd humorous account. One skipper waited until the new moon, then sped the 90 miles to Cuba, picked up six Cubans and sped the 90 miles back. He encountered no Cuban gunboats, and he encountered no United States Coast Guard as he stealthily slipped back into the Florida Keys. In fact things went so well, he just pulled up to a dock on neighbouring Key Haven, let the six, now emigrating, Cubans leisurely disembark, then the Cubans simply walked to a Chevron petrol station about a block away and dialled 911. 'Could someone come and fetch us now? We would like food, water, a new life -- and, if possible, the latest Gloria Estefan CD, *por favor.*'

(FYI: Under the 1966 Cuban Adjustment Act, also known as the 'wet foot, dry foot' policy, Cubans who reach U.S. soil are automatically granted political asylum. Cubans caught at sea, however, are typically -- and sadly -- returned to Cuba. This is why when the poor souls are intercepted within sight of land they all jump overboard and swim for their lives. If they can just make it to the beach -- dry land -- they are home free, literally.)

* * *

Gabrielle and I strolled over to Duval Street one muggy Saturday morning. There had been a violent tropical downpour a few minutes earlier and moisture was rising off the pavement.

'Look at the streets,' Gabrielle said, pointing. 'They look as if they're steaming.'

'Remember when we were in Tenerife? It was hot, but not this hot.'

'What about that time at the beach in Torquay?'

'When the Razor Fish were attacking in Paignton?'

'That time.'

'I forgot about that.'

'That too was scorching, but nothing like this.'

'Must be the humidity.'

'Let's go find some shade.'

We passed by Sloppy Joe's Bar and all the doors and windows were open and the joint was already doing a business.

'What time is it?'

'Half past nine.'

'Good to have a pub with friendly hours for topers in need of alcohol before ten in the morning.'

'Crikey, what happened to the sun sinking below the yardarm?'

'Must be five o'clock somewhere.'

We crossed Caroline Street by the Bull & Whistle (which was heaving, as well) and popped over to visit Alberto, the artist who had the open-air gallery-garden at the Porter House. Our mission was to find out where Alberto bought his framing supplies.

Alberto told us everything we needed to know about frames, mats and matting, then he introduced us to a neighbour of his in the 'garden' who also had a little open-air galley. His name was John. John resembled the footballer Zinedine, but more interestingly, John possessed the most coveted of staples -- a mat *cutter*, an industrial strength mat cutter over five-feet tall. Through island diplomacy of 'let's keep life simple and just make a trade', John agreed to let Gabrielle cut mats for our sunset photos -- gratis -- if in turn Gabrielle would cut mats for him. John had his professional mat cutter located in a miserably small shed just around the corner, but the shed had air conditioning and an AM radio. And we felt this was a monumentally good deal.

'Who's up for a cappuccino?' John asked.

We all raised our hands.

Then John looked at me. 'I'll buy if you fly.'

'Eh?'

'I'll buy if you fly, y'know, like I'll pay, if you go pick 'em up.'

I scurried off, clutching my new-found Americanism, and brought back the cappuccinos, and the four of us just sat in the shade for the next hour trying to avoid the sun, watching folk stumble out of the bars and discussing the Goldie Hawn movie called *Criss Cross* that depicted life in Key West in the '60s.

'They filmed it in 1991,' John told us, 'but other than parking some vintage Chevys on the street, and outfitting a whole lot of transients in bellbottoms, the film crew really didn't have to alter much to capture the period.'

We talked some more about what life in Key West was like back then. 'Folk were so laid-back they were nearly horizontal,' John noted. 'Life's too short to be uptight.'

About now, a patently rude customer over at John's booth bleated: 'What do I have to do to get some service around here!'

John gave us a wouldn't-you-know-it look, then slipped back over to his gallery, presumably, to give the prick a head-butt.

Alberto was a very likable bloke and we hung out with him for a while longer. Alberto, in the animated fashion of the Italians, told us all about his two little daughters, about his lovely American wife, Joan, and then about the house he and Joan had just purchased.

'We keep having girls, so we try again. *Bambini! Bambini!* We need more room. We found great old Conch house on edge of Old Town. It sorry state, but fixer-upper. Only reason can afford.'

Then Alberto jolted us with: 'We move in three weeks. *Momento!* You should take old place. It two-bedroom cottage with couple palm trees, small garden out back and plumeria tree out front. Only six-hundred dollars per month. No deposit. Include utilities.'

Gabrielle and I gave each other a look. After living in our hunchback attic, it sounded like a sprawling villa to us. Now if we could just make enough money down at the Sunset Celebration selling our sunset photos, we might be able to make it all happen.

* * *

Our first night selling photos at Mallory Square began slowly -- actually, no one showed any interest at all -- but then as the carousing tourists became more and more crocked they somehow found our photography appealing and business bloomed like the local flora. For reasons unknown to us, we grossed an astonishing sixty dollars! Imagine that. After the five-dollar evening rent for our pitch, we took home fifty-five dollars. It was a veritable fortune and we were delirious.

Over the course of the next fortnight we continued to sell sunset photos. We weren't going to get featured in the *Financial Times* doing this, but it just might give us the necessary funding to be able to move out of the attic and into Alberto's old place.

* * *

Alberto invited us to view his 'cottage' and we were very eager to see what we hoped would be our future home.

With the dizzying thoughts of a garden out back and a plumeria tree up front, we pedalled over to Duval Street, then turned left and biked up to Southard Street where we turned right and carried on for one block. Short distance to travel, long sentence. We were now at the corner of Southard and Whitehead Streets and straddling our bicycles in front of the Green Parrot.

I consulted the detailed map that Alberto had drawn for us on a sheet from his sketch pad and realised we were only a short distance from Aronovitz Lane, the narrow tropical alley down which Alberto and his family had this great cottage. Well, you can imagine our joy as we pedalled a hundred metres more along Whitehead, turned left, then dived into leafy Aronovitz Lane.

The first thing we noticed was that Aronovitz Lane was a microcosm of Key West. On the right side of the lane were tatty, dumpy, déclassé dwellings, which appeared to be on the list of 'next buildings to be condemned'.

'America sure has some rundown areas,' Gabrielle noted.

On the left side of the lane was an old two-storey Conch house with serious weather-beaten charm and next to it as you entered deeper into the lane a row of colourful, tidy cottages. Running amok in the middle of all of this was a clucking group of chickens. A hen party, perhaps?

Gabrielle and I peered up and down the passage. This we could get used to: a charming tropical lane, a romantic colourful cottage and the Green Parrot pub just around the corner. But hold on a minute! Where's Alberto's cottage? When we tried to find the correct address, it just wasn't there. How could that be? There was a 403 Aronovitz Lane and a 405 Aronovitz Lane, but no 404 Aronovitz Lane. What was going on?

I was studying the map and checking the addresses in the lane for the second time when I heard Gabrielle laugh.

'There it is!' Gabrielle pointed to the poor, pikey side of the tracks where the derelict homes stood. 'There's 404.'

We stared gobsmacked at an awful example of architecture in any part of the world. This wasn't some cosy cottage, this was a former military barracks -- and an ugly one at that (aren't they all). About now, as we were perched there squatting on our bicycles with our mouths hanging open, Alberto bounded around from the back of the shack, all smiles, and said: '*Va bene!* I see you found my cottage. Come, come for beer drinking.'

We walked around the left side of the barracks past a blooming plumeria tree and under two shady palm trees and entered a tropical backyard with a wooden deck. Always the Italian gentleman, Alberto gestured for Gabrielle to enter the 'cottage' first and Gabrielle fell through the rotting planks of the deck as she opened the back screen door.

Propping Gabrielle up, we staggered into the deep gloom of Alberto's kitchen. The kitchen was painted army green. It was the ugliest kitchen I had ever set eyes upon and my standards for these sorts of things are not high. I expected to see the chalk outline of the body left over from the crime scene. To make matters worse, the kitchen was as hot as the boiler room on a Panamanian registered trawler.

Alberto opened the door on a rusty, juddering refrigerator, handed us each a warm beer and exulted: 'Fridge come with place!' We heard a cooing sound and turned to see Alberto's wife appear out of the dark stifling depths of the barracks. Joan had a smiling kid on each hip and the entire family appeared to be very happy, healthy and content. Alberto and his family had lived in a gloomy chamber of horrors with a green kitchen for the past six years, and under close inspection, there seemed to be no short-term psychological damage. Life could only go up for them.

For us, I wasn't so sure.

Alberto gave us a tour. From the back door you stepped into the kitchen, then, curiously, from the kitchen you stepped into the bathroom, then from the bathroom you stepped into a bedroom, and then from the bedroom you stepped into another bedroom and then into the living room.

'Where are the hatches?' Gabrielle whispered.

The roof was made of tin, as are most roofs in Key West. While we were there a coconut fell off one of the palm trees and landed on the roof with such an unworldly crash, Gabrielle and I both jumped out of our flippies. We noticed that Alberto, Joan and the kids didn't even bat an eyelid.

'What you think of place?' Alberto asked, with a big smile on his face.

Always the optimist, Gabrielle said: 'Look, I can stand upright in here. Can't do that in the attic.'

'Indeed,' I added, 'we've always wanted to live in glamour-free squalor.'

With English not his mother tongue, Alberto didn't have a clue what I'd just said. Then I shot a look at Joan. Being now the mother of a two-year-old and a three-year-old, her vocabulary had dropped to less than a hundred words. She hadn't understood either.

As we moved back through the barracks, not unlike the crew moved through that submarine in the movie *Das Boat*, Alberto beamed: 'If you want I can introduce you to landlord. *Porca misera*, he's asshole, but own all cottages on this side of lane.'

* * *

Gabrielle and I were keen to upgrade our living situation, so we moved out of an attic we couldn't stand upright in and into an ex-military barracks with a green kitchen and coconuts the size of satellites falling on its tin roof. And you know what? We were never happier. Over the next month, we would take care of our chores over at the Pineapple Guest House, go snorkelling, then head down to sunset to sell our photos, then we would speed home on our bicycles and fix up the barracks.

We named it Villa Alberto.

Who in the world could stand all this joy!

There was an array of problems at our little house in paradise that had to be dealt with. Problem number one was an evil pilot light on the kitchen cooker that threw off a searing flame (think: out-of-control oil well, Iraq). The combustion accounted for the boiler-room climate in the kitchen and once we'd killed the little blighter, and the temperature in the kitchen plummeted, the quality of our lives greatly improved. Not to be outdone by technology, Gabrielle set up a small hibachi on the back deck and we barbecued -- once we'd sealed up the deck's many traps.

Our second problem was that we underestimated the tenacity of the feral chickens that shared the lane with us and awoke us at ungodly hours. Have you ever tried to get a chicken to do something it didn't want to do? Try chasing one sometime while waving an alarm clock above your head and see what happens. I can save you the trouble by telling you that you will find yourself in a lose-lose situation.

**Author's Note: There's never a dull moment down here at the end of the world, you see, feathers are flying in Key West. A portion of the populace feels the feral chickens are a sacred part of Key West's heritage and they should be allowed to range freely. Others consider the chickens a nuisance and want them removed/murdered. Here are two entries I found for you on a local web site. The web site is cannily called KEY WEST CHICKENS. The first entry is an ad, the second entry is a response on the web site's Message Board. Peck and counterpeck, if you will:

1) 'THE CHICKEN STORE is the home of the Rooster Rescue Team, a volunteer group devoted to preserving the gypsy chickens of Key West. We take in orphaned peeps, nurse sick or wounded chickens, relocate nuisance roosters and introduce the birds to visitors and children. When some newcomers wanted chickens banned from Key West, we stepped in to defend them. Do you love chickens? Do you know someone who does? Buy a Rooster Rescue T-shirt and join our Team. Help us to preserve the Soul of Old Key West.'

And now the response on the message board -- such as it was (and grammatically as it appeared):

2) 'Does anyone know just how much tourism these feathered cockroaches have killed already? Who wants to go to a place where the rent is high, the food is high and well drinks are over $6.00 a drink, then not be able to sleep or nurse a hang over? People can go to the upper Keys and stay cheaper, be closer to the Reef, drink for half price and be able to get a good night's sleep. Being able to sleep well in a Party Town is very important. So why does Key West protect these sleep killing feathered cockroaches? They should add them to Truely Nolen's (an exterminator) list of pests to be eradicated. I'll even bet that the people who want to protect these egg laying rodents don't even live in Key West. Surely no one in Key West would want to shoot themself in the foot by protecting these noisy lice carrying bag of feathers....not anyone with 2 good brain cells left in their heads. I think they should kill all of the chicken in Key West and ship both the dead chickens and the homeless up the Keys for a big chicken dinner. They can eat chickens and coconuts at no cost to the tax payers and this would solve two big parasite problems in KW.'

Well, there you have it. Card carrying, egg laying zealots.

Our third problem, and a delicate issue at that, was the bathroom. Isn't it always? When you sat on the thrown, you could look down through a hole in the floor and see the ground beneath your feet. Why covering this hole or repairing the floor had never occurred to Alberto, we don't know. The only thing we did know was it was distracting to be positioned in that oh-so private moment and be able to peep between your knees at the outside world and watch the chickens go by. I guess some twisted side to me was always expecting the postman to pop his head up through there and announce that he had a Special Delivery. You can make up your own joke as what to say in response.

Our fourth problem was the termites.

We are slowly learning the hungry little buggers have insatiable appetites (not unlike that bloke down the pub on Wednesday Curry Night). You see, many of the homes -- including the Pineapple Guest House -- were built with Dade County pine. Dade County is the county Miami is located in, remember? And Dade County pine is an impressively hearty pine, so bulletproof and durable in fact I remember trying to drive a nail into the wall at Popcorn Joe's one day and the nail just bending. I did a little research for you and found out that Dade County pine has been almost completely harvested and no longer grows in commercial quantities. Many of South Florida's oldest buildings were built with Dade County pine, so whenever one of those buildings is torn down, folks in the know try to reclaim its timbers and flooring for reuse.

We did not have Dade County pine in Villa Alberto, so the shelves in our bathroom, and what was left of our closest in our bedroom, had long served as lunch for Key West's voracious termites. In need of financial support to administer repair, Gabrielle and I biked over to see our landlord. I won't mention his name, but for literary purposes let's just call him Mr Tosser.

Mr Tosser -- who sported a comb-over that would impress the likes of even Robert Robinson -- had posh offices over in a large refurbished building in an exclusive part of Key West known as Truman Annex (named after President Truman who maintained his 'holiday White House' there). And the man (Mr Tosser, not Truman) had made his money from strips joints located out on North Roosevelt Boulevard (Goldie Hawn played the part of a stripper in Criss Cross, by the way.)

Anyway, where was I? Oh, yeah, Mr Tosser was all smiles when we paid him our first month's rent, but this time around when we asked for assistance in the form of some paint and a few scraps of wood, he had metamorphosed into a slum landlord -- with a condescending attitude.

'Forget any wood. I'm not about to rebuild the place. I'll pay for one gallon of paint. That's it. Nothing more.'

Gabrielle gave this ill-bred creature a long look: 'One gallon of paint won't even do a first coat on half the kitchen.'

'One gallon,' he shot back, lighting a cigar and putting his flat feet up on his desk. 'Take it or leave it.'

Gabrielle forged on. 'We're not asking you to pay us to paint the place or take any money off the rent, we just want to live in a comfortable clean house. Besides it will improve the value.'

Our slum landlord fixed us with a withering look and actually cackled: 'Then I'd have to raise your rent...'

Tosser.

Gabrielle was fuming as we left our landlord's sickly plush, well-painted offices. As we passed by his secretary in the outer office, we could tell that the secretary had heard it all and she was embarrassed by the way we had been treated.

When we stepped outside and unchained our bicycles from a palm tree, Gabrielle hissed: 'The bastard! Did you see how he talked down to us?'

We pedalled over to the beach at Fort Zack and went for a swim. It's amazing what a nice dip in the sea can do for one's state of mind. When we splashed out of the water, the sand felt hot on our feet and good between our toes. We slapped on some suntan lotion, grabbed our masks and snorkels and went right back in.

When we came back out of the salty Atlantic for the second time, we saw Shark-Man standing there holding a machete and a coconut.

'Hello, my good friends,' he bellowed. 'How 'bout some cool coconut milk?'

Shark-Man demonstrated the delicate art of slicing open a coconut while holding it between his bare feet. We drank the rich, cool milk, then just hung out with Shark-Man for a while. How can people on this earth be so different? How come the guy with all the money is a flaming arsehole, but the bloke with no money is a gentleman?

We asked Shark-Man if he had heard of our landlord, and he just said: 'Oh, that sumbitch. Everyone knows all about him. Has an inferiority complex and a hydra for a wife.'

We told Shark-Man about our encounter. Shark-Man went silent for a moment and regarded the machete resting on the sand near his feet. Then he said: 'If he gives you anymore grief let me know and I'll make sure he ends up with a horse's head in his bed like that asswipe in the movie the *Godfather*.'

Gabrielle and I had a good laugh -- but then we stopped, and do you know why? That's when we realised Shark-Man was not joking.

* * *

After showering at the outdoor shower at the beach, we both felt revived and refreshed. Gabrielle went off to the shed to cut mats and listen to the 'Fishing Report' on AM radio. And I decided to have a surprise waiting for Gabrielle when she returned home.

I pedalled over to the paint shop on White Street and purchased two throwaway brushes, a roller, a pan, a can of blue spray paint and three gallons of off-white paint (anything other than magnolia), then I sped back home with all these coveted items balancing precariously in the basket of my bike. Have you ever tried to ride a bicycle with, say, a small child or large animal or three gallons of off-white paint shifting in the basket? No easy trick, is it? You try to turn left and the bike takes you right. You endeavour to pedal in a straight line and the bike wants to slalom. I feared I would be stopped for biking under the influence, but I stuck to the back alleys and tropical lanes and I made it home without catching the eye of Key West's finest.

It took me a couple of hours to apply a lonely coat of low-end-of-the-market paint on the ceiling, walls and door jams of the kitchen. The remnants of the army green were still visible as a government-issue hue beneath the fresh coat but it greatly freshened the kitchen and lightened up what had been a deeply gloomy part of the house. Then I spray painted the kitchen table to make it fresh and vibrant.

Besides the cracking fridge, Alberto had left us his old blender when he had moved out, so I hustled over to Fausto's Market on Fleming Street and purchased rich peaches and luscious pears and fresh-squeezed orange juice and creamy coconut juice and even a few ripening bananas. Then I slalomed my way back home and threw everything in the blender. I had never used a blender before, so you can imagine my joy at the chance to concoct a tropical no-name drink for my main squeeze.

I jammed the top on the blender, took a deep breath and stabbed 'High'. And guess what? The richest, thickest ooze was born and I watched in childlike wonder as the spawn metamorphosed into a roiling maelstrom and then, not unlike that volcano in Monserrat, exploded out the top of the blender and spewed a warm hue all over our freshly painted kitchen. Being inexperienced with blenders, I had failed to maintain a grip on the bloody top.

And, Sod's law, two seconds later Gabrielle returned from cutting mats. And when she saw the state of the kitchen, she screamed with laughter: 'I like what you've done with the place! Can't believe you found magnolia in America!'

* * *

It was now Spring Break. And business was picking up at the Pineapple Guest House. Have you heard about the rite of passage called Spring Break? It's that time of year when university students from all over America head for the sun to disrobe and pickle their brains for weeks on end with alcohol purchased with fake IDs.

It coincides with mating season.

If Popcorn Joe was out running errands (read: in the hunt for members of the opposite sex), Gabrielle and I would take up the slack and deal with the new arriving guests. On one occasion, I remember a group of coeds from the University of Wisconsin had checked into the guest house. There were 12 young lasses in total and they rented four apartments. The next day, however, Gabrielle and I had to laugh. Just before the crack of noon, the holidaymakers awoke and hastened to the swimming pool so they could go back to sleep, but there weren't 12 topless young ladies, now there were 24. They had multiplied (not in the biblical sense, mind you) during the night.

As the week went on the numbers seemed to increase exponentially (everyone was sleeping in shifts now), but when it came time for the Spring Breakers to check out the following Saturday, the number had magically been reduced back down to the original 12.

A single sunburnt, burnt-out representative from each apartment dragged her wasted carcass up to the back deck where Gabrielle and I were sipping our morning con leche with Popcorn Joe.

'You can come and view the apartments now,' the quartet intoned in unison.

'Did you enjoy your Spring Break in Key West?' Gabrielle asked the noticeably subdued university students.

'Going to have to take a vacation when we get back home to recover from this vacation.'

'Where did you hang out?' I asked.

'Rick's. That place rocks,' said a Lindsay Lohan factory reject.

'Long lines to get in, though,' added Paris. 'I'd pee my pants before I'd lose my place in line.'

'That's commitment,' Gabrielle said.

'Were there any good parties?' Joe asked.

'Shit, yeah,' one coed said, 'but we weren't allowed in.'

'Why not?'

'You had to have a partner?'

'And?'

The young lady blushed and turned to a friend. 'You tell 'em.'

'No, like you tell 'em.'

'Nooo, like you tell 'em.'

'Okay. Okay. Chill. Like I'll tell 'em... The girls were blindfolded and they had to guess if it was their boyfriend or a stranger.'

'Doing what?'

'Doing it.'

'Doing it?'

'Yeah, doing it. You know, like...ah...penetrating.'

When we regained consciousness, I accompanied Gabrielle to each apartment, and we expected the worst, but other than an old doobie in one of the ashtrays and a thong in a banana tree, the apartments and compound appeared in good nick and refitting wouldn't be necessary -- this year.

* * *

After Spring Break was over (and the rape-me-fuck-me-beat-me-suck-me bacchanal skin-fest was history for another year), I ran into Captain Jerry again. I was watering the large travelling palm located in the front of the guest house, when I spotted a transient rifling through our post box. The transient couldn't see me as I was completely blocked by the travelling palm. If you don't know what a travelling palm looks like, now is the time to tell you. Imagine a Flamenco dancer's fan sticking out of the ground. Now imagine a Flamenco dancer's fan that is over 20 feet tall and more than ten feet wide.

I continued to observe the transient and that's when I realised this benign vagabond looked familiar. Standing there was the bloke who had politely requested thirty-seven cents in chapter one.

I put the hose-pipe down and approached Captain Jerry.

'Just checking to see if I have any mail,' he offered. 'As you've probably guessed, I live rough. Don't have anywhere to get my mail. Sometimes I get a shitload from home, so Popcorn Joe lets me get it here.'

'Sounds okay by me,' I said, then I went back to watering the plants.

Captain Jerry turned to walk away, then stopped and turned just like Colombo used to do on TV. 'Say, could I possibly borrow thirty-seven cents?'

I already had a dollar out of my pocket. 'What do you need it for, stamps?'

'Stamps! Are you shitting me? It's going toward my first beer of the day.'

Captain Jerry was an interesting bloke: He was not of humble origins, rather from an upper-crust New England family, and his accent reflected his upbringing. He was university educated, hugely astute, could speak on any subject from Shakespeare to the intricacies of hacking into the Pentagon, yet for unknown reasons he had embarked on a successful albeit inert career of unemployment and alcohol abuse. Not one to squander good beer money on rent, Captain Jerry told me he resided in the crawl space under a neighbouring house owned by a colourful couple named Don and Shirley.

'Why don't you get your mail at Don and Shirley's?'

'They don't like me hanging around after sunrise. They rent a few rooms, and even though I have wisdom to dispense, I frighten the guests. So I repair late and slip away early.'

Captain Jerry was one of the characters that we dealt with from time to time at the guest house, but there was another character worth mentioning. And her name was Betty.

Betty was a zaftig once-attractive woman, with terrifying cleavage, well past her mental health sell-by date, who resided in her car parked by the Historic Seaport ('affordable housing' in Key West is the back of your car). Betty also used the guest house as her local address as she needed somewhere to pick up her welfare cheque. Rumour had it that Betty had come to Key West to enrich her gap year and never left, but that was not the peculiar thing. The curious bit about Betty was that she always dressed somewhat elegantly. And she had wigs, lots of them (more than Cher even), and we never knew what colour her hair would be from one day to the next. One early evening, Gabrielle and I passed by her 'boat of a car', a Buick -- big by even American standards -- and she was pretty much stark-naked in the backseat with her arse up in the air, changing clothes and all, struggling with boas and a thong, preparing to turn herself loose on unsuspecting Key West. Late in the evening, Betty could be found cruising Duval Street, bosoms decamping from a low-cut top, hoping for an invitation to, say, dinner, from, say, a mental-health professional.

Did I say Betty was a hooker? I didn't say Betty was a hooker. But she certainly lived by the bent adage: 'If you got it -- or once had it -- flaunt what you've got left of it.'

* * *

It's Sunday morning. Early. Still dark out. And the phone is ringing. And ringing. And ringing. I peer bleary eyed (and without the benefit of my contacts) at our lonely alarm clock. The illuminated blur reads 6:00 a.m. Who's calling at this hour?

I answer. 'This better be good.'

'It is,' comes a gruff, booming voice. This is the Department of Homeland Security...'

Shit!

I hiss at Gabrielle, 'It's Immigration!'

Caught decidedly off guard and not knowing what else to do, I blurt out: 'They don't live here anymore. Please leave a message after the beep. BEEEP!'

Then I hear laughter. Lots of laugher. And I recognised that laugh.

'Rubin? Is that you? That's your best one yet and I hate you for it!'

Our dear friend, John Rubin, practical joker extraordinaire, was up to his usual tricks. Rubin is from Manchester, and he was coming to the Keys to do some deep-sea fishing. His passion. That and real ale. I told him about the Pineapple Guest House and Popcorn Joe and how he could stay in the 'efficiency' if he bought lots of beer.

'Consider it done.'

I hung up the receiver and looked over at my sleepy wife. 'You go back to sleep. I'm going to go buy the Mullet Wrap.'

Unshaven and scruffy, I slipped out of Villa Alberto into the predawn morning and headed over to the corner of Southard and Duval to procure the morning paper from a predatory vending machine. I inserted two quarters but then yanked too hard on the little handle and the spring-loaded door snapped at me like that till in *Open All Hours*. And I lost the two quarters. I searched my pockets. No more quarters, just a rogue dollar bill. I needed to make change, but no establishments were open.

I plodded down Duval Street in the direction of the Bull & Whistle and saw a group of well-dressed tourists -- early morning folk from a different time zone -- talking too loudly, coming my way. A cruise ship must be in. I approached the *tourons* and said these words: 'Anybody got any change?'

Well, with me being unshaven, tanned black and not dressed in my best togs, one well-to-do passenger look me up and down and said: 'Well, go on, then. How much do *you* want? The last guy asked us for thirty-seven cents!'

On account of my venture into transient-dom, Gabrielle and I didn't have a chance to take a peek at the Mullet Wrap until we were sitting out on the back deck with Popcorn Joe having our morning *con leche*. Joe took a sip of his coffee and then handed me the Mullet Wrap. He tapped with an index finger at a certain article on the front page. I read and Gabrielle peeped over my shoulder.

Seems there had been a shooting at Rick's Bar on Duval Street the night before:

A 21-YEAR-OLD MAN FROM NEIGHBOURING STOCK ISLAND WAS ARRESTED AND CHARGED WITH TWO COUNTS OF ATTEMPTED MURDER AFTER HE ALLEGEDLY PULLED OUT A HANDGUN AND SHOT TWO PATRONS ON THE SECOND-FLOOR DANCE FLOOR OF RICK'S. THE BULLET ENTERED ONE FELLOW'S NECK, EXITED HIS CHEEK AND THEN HIT THE SECOND FELLOW, LODGING IN HIS SKULL. ONE OF THE VICTIMS UNDERWENT SURGERY AFTER BEING AIRLIFTED TO RYDER TRAUMA CENTER IN MIAMI. HE REMAINS IN CRITICAL CONDITION.

THE INCIDENT APPEARED TO HAVE NO NEGATIVE EFFECT ON BUSINESS, AS A TRADEMARK LONG LINE OF WAITING CUSTOMERS EXTENDED OUTSIDE OF RICK'S SATURDAY NIGHT.

CHAPTER 9

Someone stole our bikes.

Our bikes had been parked in the back garden. They had been there the night before leaning against one of the palm trees. Now they were gone.

Our bikes were old, beaten-up and rusty. We loved our bikes. We went everywhere on them. We used them to pick up groceries, or deliver film to Pro Photo or commute to the Pineapple Guest House a few minutes away. And we used them to get to the beach. We had bonded with our bikes. We had become one. And we were outraged.

'I'm going to call the police,' I said.

'No!'

'Why not?'

'We don't want to bring attention to ourselves. If the police find out we've overstayed our visas, they'll deport us.'

'What do we do then?'

'Let's talk to our neighbours instead. Perhaps someone spotted something.'

The first person we spoke to was our neighbour to our left, an African American gentleman by the name of Vincent. All of Vincent's friends called him 'Snake', so we called him Snake, as well.

'I smoked a little reefer and drank a lot of Southern Comfort,' Snake told us. 'I was pretty fucked-up. Sorry, man, didn't see a thing.'

We thanked Snake and struck out to corner Snake's neighbour, one ramshackle shack over. This fellow was known in the lane as the 'Pig-Man' on account of the Vietnamese potbellied pig he kept as a pet. (A pet of a certain stink, might I add.) Pig-Man, who had a pope's face, but a sinner's disposition, told us that he 'helped close the Green Parrot and had been lucky to find my way the half-block back home'. And, no, he hadn't seen or heard anything suspicious as he had passed out in the garden while in the process of nitrogenating one of his palm trees. We thanked the Pig-Man for his time (and the details) and pressed on.

We stayed on the poor side of the tracks and interviewed an elderly Bahamian fellow two barracks to our right. I can't remember this gentleman's name, but I do remember he had liquid doe-brown eyes and only one leg. 'I can't go anywhere because of this fricken' leg,' he shouted, 'so I was home all night long.'

'Did you hear anything suspicious?' Gabrielle asked.

'EH?' the old man bellowed. 'WHAT DID YOU SAY?'

Gabrielle and I shifted our investigation to the upmarket side of the tropical lane. The first person we spoke to was Mrs Grace. 'Grace' was just her first name, but everybody in the lane called her Mrs Grace as a show of respect. Mrs Grace was of Cuban descent, *muy simpatica* and had resided in the lane since birth. We asked her if she had seen any suspicious activity the night before and she said that she had. Then she added: 'I see suspicious activity in this lane *every* night!'

We tried to speak to Mrs Grace's nephews -- one lived in the quaint cottage next door and the other in that two-storey Conch house with weather-beaten charm, but one was at work and the other in jail.

So we spoke to Mrs Grace's neighbour on the other side. A porcine, repellently insufferable minger in her thirties who thought she was quite important (she was a hostess at a bad restaurant on the neighbouring island). And guess what? This silly bovine was condescending.

'What do you expect?' she said. 'Look where you live.' And then she shut the door in our faces.

Stay tuned on this front.

The last cottage on the rich side of the lane was owned by a taxicab driver (think Sting, on a bad day) and his Cuban wife (think Meatloaf, on a good day). The wife, who looked as if she hadn't missed many meals, flogged -- and I tell no porkies here -- the latest weight-reducing plan. The husband did the taxi thing and sold drugs on the side.

'We were both pretty wasted last night,' hubby told us. 'I'm a motor-mouth when I'm on coke, so I was preaching loud and long about a lot of things that I know nothing about. Sorry, didn't hear a damn thing.'

'What about your wife?' I asked.

'Mary Jane brownies and Cherry Garcia,' was what he said, and I guess that said it all.

When we returned to Villa Alberto, Snake was sitting in the shade under the plumeria tree.

'Was Michelle rude to you?'

'Who's Michelle?'

'That slut across the street who closed the door on you. Had friends over once, so I parked my pickup in front of her house. She reamed me out, then took her garden hose and sprayed my ass good. Said nobody was allowed to park in front of her house except her. People like that frighten me.'

I stared across the lane at Michelle's house. Sad. This lovely tropical lane was loaded with loaded characters -- and one bad bovine.

* * *

The Conch Republic Independence Celebration is here! Yes, you heard right. This is the time of the year when locals pay homage to their 'homeland', the Conch Republic. It also gives Key Westers another chance to lure the tourist dollar and justify a drinking problem.

To fully understand the Conch Republic, you must be au fait with its charter. In a never-ending effort to educate, I have scribbled it here for you, such as it is: 'DEDICATED TO THE FUNDAMENTALLY AMERICAN SPIRIT OF A PEOPLE UNAFRAID TO STAND UP TO "GOVERNMENT GONE MAD WITH POWER" THAT EMBODIED THE FOUNDING OF THE CONCH REPUBLIC IN 1982. AS THE WORLD'S FIRST FIFTH WORLD NATION, A SOVEREIGN STATE OF MIND SEEKING ONLY TO BRING MORE HUMOR, WARMTH, AND RESPECT TO A WORLD IN SORE NEED OF ALL THREE, THE CONCH REPUBLIC REMAINS THE COUNTRY WHO SECEDED WHERE OTHERS FAILED.'

As you can well imagine, this is a joyous time of the year to be in Key West. There's much to do, and much of it is for charity (Decadence for a Cause, you might say).

So as to give you an idea of the various happenings, I have chosen to list a few of the fun events over the ten-day celebration:

FRIDAY

7 PM -- The Kick Off Party at the Schooner Wharf Bar...Conch Shell Blowing Contest with Prizes, Music, Food and Fun.

SATURDAY

12 PM -- THE GREAT CONCH REPUBLIC DRAG RACE -- featuring drag queens -- sponsored by 801 Bourbon Bar and Bourbon Street Pub (**Author's Note: These are gay bars)

8 PM -- Conch Republic Royal Family Investiture Party at The Green Parrot Bar -- Come help elect this year's Conch Republic Royal Family.

SUNDAY

8 PM -- THE GRAND CONCH REPUBLIC MILITARY AND AMBASSADOR'S BALL.

MONDAY - REST DAY -- (there's a big week coming up).

THURSDAY

8 PM -- The US 1 Radio 104.1 FM 'World's Longest Parade' down Duval Street from the Atlantic Ocean to the Gulf of Mexico at the Schooner Wharf Bar (**Author's Note: In reality the parade is only about a mile long, but it's 'from one "ocean" to another'.

FRIDAY

7 PM -- The Conch Republic Naval Parade and Great Battle for the Conch Republic. This is THE event of the Celebration. Best viewing from the Ocean Key House Resort, Mallory Square and the Key West Hilton. (**Author's Note: This is a water fight between local craft and the mighty United States Coast Guard. We have dinghies, Jet-Skis and water balloons. They have a 200-foot cutter with radar, a powerful water cannon and a sober crew. Gabrielle and I watched the battle from Mallory Dock along with thousands upon thousands of other delirious folk. And we got wet. Soaked-through gloriously wet.)

SATURDAY

ALL MORNING -- Great American, Florida and Monroe County Cleanup in the Conch Republic -- help keep the Florida Keys beautiful (**Author's Note: Everybody gets together and cleans up litter off beaches, parks and surrounding areas. Gabrielle and I helped clean the beach by the White Street pier. Do this once and you'll never litter anywhere, ever, again.)

4 PM -- The 19th Annual Conch Republic Bed Race...to benefit AIDS Help, Inc. THE MOST FUN YOU CAN HAVE IN BED WITH YOUR CLOTHES ON! (**Author's Note: no more Author's Notes.)

The Conch Republic Days reeled in schools of tourists at a time of the year when tourism had been just about all fished out. And kegs of money were raised for charity.

Business was booming at the Pineapple Guest House and Popcorn Joe, in a charitable mood, surprised us with new, used bikes. Both bikes were beaten-up, rusty and painted black to conceal original ownership.

* * *

Gabrielle and I decided to treat ourselves to dinner.

We chose the Mobster Lobster Restaurant. This curiously named themed eatery is set in an open-air tropical jungle. And it's known for its period decor and array of fine seafood. More importantly, it was conveniently located on Duval Street and just beyond the end of our tropical lane.

The location was an attractive consideration. We could consume alcohol and not have to use our bikes to convey back home (folk get arrested in Key West, riding a bike, drunk).

We strolled around the block to the entrance on Duval Street and -- you won't believe this -- walking straight towards us were two long-lost friends of ours from back home, Sally and Ian.

'Sally! Ian! What are you doing here?'

'We were at a tennis tournament in Miami. Just popped down for the day. What are you two doing here?'

We told Sally and Ian about our plunge into adventure and a new life, and Ian said: 'Jammy buggers. Want to hear all about this.'

Gabrielle and I had purchased our wedding rings from Ian, but we had lost contact for a few years. Strange to run into them way down here at the end of the world's longest dead-end street.

'We were just about to go to dinner. Peckish?'

'Could eat a cow,' Sally said.

We led Ian and Sally to the entrance of the Mobster Lobster, then realised there really was no entrance, more of a passage between two buildings. We peered into gloomy depths with good music and entered a hidden garden patio with a canopy of trees.

The hidden garden had a square bar in the middle. Since we were now celebrating with friends, we decided to slake our thirst at the square bar before being seated. The temperature was 80 degrees and we all wore shorts. It seemed strange to sit outside with shorts on, at night, in April.

Our bartender, Mitch, was from Boston. Mitch wore a T-shirt with these words on the front: YOU ARE NOTHING IF YOU DON'T **BELIEVE** IN SOMETHING. When Mitch turned around to fetch our drinks, these words were on the back: I **BELIEVE** I WILL HAVE ANOTHER BEER!

For reasons unknown to us, Mitch felt compelled to tell all of us his life story. He had moved to Key West with his wife of five years. Shortly after arriving in the Keys, his wife fell in love and ran off with another -- woman. Yes, you heard right. One thing about Key West, it tends to bring out the real you.

Mitch said it had been a serious blow to his confidence and was wreaking havoc with his masculinity. Gabrielle and I looked at Sally and Ian. Ian and Sally looked back at us. We shared a silent moment with loud subtext, then ordered more drinks.

I had met Ian, a jeweller, when I was teaching skiing in Kitzbühel, Austria (that's another story, another book). Then Gabrielle and I married in Kitzbühel, and it made romantic sense to procure our wedding rings from Ian. Just to make this more bizarre, Sally and Ian had honeymooned in Key West in 1989 and that's why they had returned today to see if much had changed. Other than us living there, they said it seemed nothing had changed at all.

'How'd you manage a work permit, Gabrielle?' Ian asked.

'Don't ask,' Gabrielle said, looking around to make sure no one had heard.

After a few beverages, the music increased in volume. We turned our attention to a small stage under a big leafy tree. A duet was playing. The duet consisted of two sinister-looking Russian guitarists. They played melodic Zhivago-esque strains on balalaikas and occasionally they sang in Russian, and it was all very moody and romantic, and didn't fit in at all with this tropical environment. But nobody seemed to mind. And we didn't either. We just enjoyed being there with our dear friends Sally and Ian, and we felt good about our new life at Villa Alberto -- in a backwater tropical lane chocka with weirdoes.

A comforting aspect of Key West is, no matter how weird or arresting or nonconformist you may be, you will fit in, you see, there will always be somebody there more unconventional and wackier than you.

We eventually repaired to a table in a leafy corner and shortly thereafter an androgynous waitress walked up with our menus and handed one menu each to Sally, Ian and me -- and two to Gabrielle. The waitress (who told us it was her/his first day) realised her/his multiple-menu mistake and apologised.

'No worries,' Gabrielle teased. 'I'm a big eater.'

We studied the menus, all of them, then had a peep around the garden restaurant. The cuisine may have been seafood, but the theme was dramatically gangsters and mobsters. Perhaps the Russian connection made good sense after all.

I can't remember too much more about that evening other than the placed 'filled to the gills', and we all ate some sort of rubbery slimy creature and drank an inordinate amount of wine, but one thing I do remember is that the restaurant had a resident cat. A black cat with a white moustache and white paws that made it look as if he were wearing spats. Just like a gangster. The cat, for obvious and sound reasons, hung out near the kitchen, but he would also make the rounds and visit the tables. For unknown reasons, he decided to spend much of the evening with us.

Mitch stopped by our table from time to time (to update his CV) and informed us the cat's name was Mr Leroy. We all concurred that the name suited the feline perfectly.

When the evening was over, we bid farewell to Sally and Ian and promised to get together with them back in the UK if we were deported, then Mitch led us to the kitchen -- said we could slip out the back way. This meant passing *through* the kitchen. Passing through kitchens with territorial cooks has never been my idea of a good time, but the cooks were all stoned and they just grinned goofily at us as we penetrated their purple-haze domain and slipped out into serene and peaceful Aronovitz Lane.

But Aronovitz Lane wasn't serene and peaceful tonight, all hell was breaking loose. Some careless sod had parked a bright blue Jeep directly in front of the Bitch-Bovine's house, and she was going off the deep end, yelling and screaming insanely at anyone and everyone who dared enter the lane. In fact, the Bitch-Bovine was putting on such a show, the taxi cab driver/pusher and his weight-watching wife had brought out folding chairs so they could enjoy the carnage from the front row.

Even Mrs Grace was observing the fireworks from her porch swing just on the other side.

About now, Mitch appeared: 'See that blue Jeep? That belongs to the manager of our restaurant. He parked it there, innocently, and now that witch is going to blow a gasket.'

And she did. The Bitch-Bovine took out her hosepipe and inserted it through the open window on the passenger side of the Jeep and proceeded to irrigate the jeep's interior. And when the manager of the Mobster Lobster came running out to protest, he was hosed, as well.

The Bitch-Bovine was dangerously close to becoming the emotional equivalent of the *Perfect Storm*. Gabrielle and I were afraid to attempt the crossing to our house, so we came about, tacked back through the restaurant and sailed completely around the block.

That night we went to bed late and I had schizzed out dreams. I dreamt there had been a raging storm on the island and that all the power had been knocked out. Key West lay in darkness and on account of the blackness an evil side of me surfaced unbidden. A side that wanted revenge for the little people. In my merlot-induced dream, I dreamt that I had slipped across the street -- under cloak of drunkenness -- and spray painted the Bitch-Bovine's brand new black BMW.

I remember waking bolt upright in the middle of the night, soaked in sweat. It's frightening how real dreams can be and I slept fitfully until the next morning when I awoke to the smell of robust Cuban coffee. Gabrielle had brought me a cup of Cafe Cubano (made from Pilon espresso) in bed.

I had a few sips of coffee and felt much better, except for the hangover, of course. I rose and yawned my way into the kitchen. Gabrielle was mashing various types of fruit in a big bowel, creating some magical tropical juice.

My wife gave me a big, warm smile, then I asked her: 'Why aren't you using the blender?'

And Gabrielle came back with these haunting words: 'Power's still out.'

I shot Gabrielle a look, then pulled back the kitchen curtain and peered, horrified, outside. Across the lane, right in front of the Bitch-Bovine's house, was a Key West police car, bright red and blue lights flashing. The Bitch-Bovine was standing there gesticulating in a deranged fashion and some poor cop was feverishly writing screeds on a clipboard. Seems some demented soul had done a Picasso in bright blue paint all over the bonnet and windscreen and down along the side of her precious, overpriced 528i. The fledgling artist must have been going through his Blue Period.

While the cop was busy taking the report (and the verbal abuse), I snuck across and paid a clandestine visit to Mrs Grace -- Mrs Grace who sees all that goes on in the lane.

And do you know what Mrs Grace told me? She said that everyone knew it had been the manager of the restaurant who had spray painted the BMW.

'It's obvious, isn't it? That paint is exactly the same colour as the manager's jeep. It had to be him. That's what everyone is saying.'

Then, as I started to walk away, Mrs Grace froze me with: 'Awful storm last night. Couldn't sleep. With no power, my air conditioner didn't work. Had to sit out on the porch in the dark all night long.' And then: 'My neighbour may be my neighbour, but I think she made her own bed, and if you make your bed, you have to sleep in it.'

And then Mrs Grace winked at me.

* * *

Remember that episode of *Men Behaving Badly*, the one where they holiday down at the seaside in Worthing? And they get really pissed? And then the next morning they wake up and can't remember what they'd got up to the night before? And they don't know why there's a gigantic fake fish in their hotel room?

That's it.

Just wanted to know if you remembered.

CHAPTER 10

Shortly after I returned from Mrs Grace's, Gabrielle burst into the bathroom -- where I was emptying the contents of a sachet of Resolve into a glass of water -- and sombrely announced: 'Someone's at the door. For you.'

You can imagine my sincere horror as I slunk through Villa Alberto and headed for the door. I was certain it was the Key West police.

But it wasn't.

It was Mr Leroy.

'I think you've made a friend,' Gabrielle said.

I opened the screen door for Mr Leroy, then fetched him a bowl of water.

Mr Leroy lapped contentedly at the water for a long time, then gazed up at me for a moment and bolted straight into the bowels of the house.

Laughing, Gabrielle and I ran after him and found him in the middle of our bed.

'Now what are you going to do?' Gabrielle said.

I just smiled. 'How did he know where the bed was? He made a beeline.'

From that day on, Mr Leroy became part of our family. And his modus operandi was always the same: sit quietly on the other side of the screen door until we noticed him, have a drink of water and then bolt for the bed.

Mr Leroy had a little nick out of his ear and it always worried us that he lived a secret life of back-alley violence. But then one day we saw an officer from the Key West equivalent of the RSPCA patrolling our lane. I whisked Mr Leroy into my arms to protect him and the officer yelled over: 'Oh, don't worry about him. That cat's been taken care of.'

I asked the officer what she meant and she informed me that the Key West Humane Society, as it's called, is humane, indeed. When a stray cat is found, the arresting officer takes the homeless creature back to the 'pound' and instead of euthanizing it, she gives the little lost beast all its shots, a soothing flea bath and then returns the fury animal to its fishy free-range life on the street with a little souvenir: a scar where it'd been neutered and a tiny nick out of the tip of an ear to show anyone who may happen upon the cat that it's already had that all-important free veterinary care.

If you are a cat, and don't have a nice family to take care of you, there are worse places to live than feline-friendly Key West.

* * *

Key West has its fair share of theft.

Our bikes were stolen, that you know already. And the odd car gets stolen. And really anything that's not bolted down gets pinched. You simply can not leave anything in an open garage door or on the sidewalk in front of your house such as garden tools, a ladder, a hosepipe or even a chair that you've been sitting on reading the Mullet Wrap until that damn phone rang and you had to go inside to answer it.

Yes, anything and everything in Key West gets nicked, but having said that, none of us ever thought that someone would try to steal the 55-foot glass-bottom boat.

Here's what happened:

The *Fireball*, one of Key West's venerable tourist attractions, was berthed at the Ocean Key Resort & Spa at the foot of Duval Street. In the middle of the night, the maritime equivalent of John Robie boarded the *Fireball*, pussyfooted around and then broke in. It may have been the middle of the night, but not many people are asleep in Key West in the middle of the night. You see, at the precise moment the perpetrator was gaining entry, a young lady staying in a third-floor suite at the Ocean Key came out on the balcony to smoke some ditchweed. Our dutiful citizen, who believed devoutly in law and order -- when it didn't pertain to her -- put down her skunk, picked up the phone and called police.

And the police arrived just in time to see John Robie fire up the *Fireball*.

'Shut it down!' yelled one of the officers.

But our soon-to-be felon didn't comply (they never do, do they?), rather he threw the powerful diesel engines into 'all ahead full', and as the sleek *Fireball* shot forward, she summarily ripped all the surrounding pilings out of the harbour bottom. In his addled attempt at flight, our impatient thief had failed to remember one of boating's foremost rules: ALWAYS UNTIE THE VESSEL BEFORE LEAVING PORT!'

'You're under arrest!' shouted the cop.

Defiant to the end, and not about to take orders from THE MAN, our hell-bent interloper pursued his only remaining avenue of escape -- he jumped overboard and started to swim.

The police tried, but try as they might, they could not lure John Robie out of the warm Gulf waters. They threatened him, and they tried to coax him, but he was having none of it.

Yes, nothing was working until a tarpon broke the surface near where our lad with a decision-making disorder was now treading water. And then the situation changed and it changed fast. And it all happened because an in-the-know

Key West police officer had grown up in the Florida Keys and he knew these waters, and he knew the size of this fish, and all he had to do was yell: 'Shark!' and the now washed-up malefactor was out of the water and beached faster than you could say: 'You should have stayed in school and studied Ichthyology.'

For those of you who don't know what tarpon are, perhaps I should tell you. Tarpon are premier saltwater game fish that inhabit the flats and can often be found in the harbour. And they are big, seriously big. You can go down to the glass-bottom boat on any given evening (unless it's being taken for a joyride to Cuba) and see tarpon crest the water right there in the shallow, clear harbour -- impressive, for a five- to seven-foot beast.

* * *

Gabrielle's mother is visiting. 'Doris' has never been to America before. Let alone Florida. Let alone Key West. She can't get over the American accents. And the air conditioning. Or the heat. Every time she steps outdoors she's taken by the fact that it's warmer outdoors than indoors. And she utters 'Oh, dear.' Doris has only read about America. And seen it portrayed in *Fraser, Friends* and *Desperate Housewives*. And by Louis Theroux. So she walks around gobsmacked a lot.

Doris has just purchased a bathing costume. Something she hasn't done for forty years. And now she has a face that's scorched from spending too long in the tropical sun her first time around -- fifteen minutes.

* * *

I do not have a green thumb. I apparently have a black thumb. I kill plants. When plants see me coming they throw their fronds in the air as if I'm holding a pistil to their stigma (I know, I know, not that amusing, but I learnt about pistils and stigmas in university and have been waiting yonks to put it to use somewhere).

Gabrielle, on the other hand, has a radiantly green thumb. Inherited it from her mother. Plants love Gabrielle. She talks to them. Plays Cuban music to them. Even cuddles them. Gabrielle and Doris are now outside in the backyard planting hibiscus and frangipani, festooning Villa Alberto in tropical flora.

And I've been banned from the garden and exiled to the bathroom where I'm now cleaning the tub.

Our bathtub has footprints in it. Every bathtub in Key West has footprints in it because we walk around barefoot half the time. Curiously, our bathtub has footprints -- and some tiny paw prints.

Green only with envy, I peek out the back screen door. Gabrielle is now planting a pineapple, the top of it, actually. Popcorn Joe taught her how to do this. What you do is cut the part off a pineapple that looks like a cartoon character's hair, cut away the excess flesh (so it won't rot), let it dry outdoors for a few days, then plant it and let Mother Nature take over: plenty of light and plenty of warmth and better dry than drowned in water. You will soon grow your own little pineapple bush and one day you will see a plump pineapple rising from the spiky leaves.

Wait! What's this? I'm being called outside. Gabrielle needs me! Says there's a gardening chore she wants me to take care of. Just when I reckoned I'd been relegated, never to appear in the garden Premiership again, I'm wanted by the big guns.

Gabrielle has a rickety old wooden ladder and she has it leaned up against the side of the house. And now she's pointing at the large palm tree that holds sway over our tin roof. The palm tree is pregnant with heavily laden coconuts that just can't wait to go Bombs Away! on our tin roof in the middle of the night. Now I'm being handed a curious looking instrument that we borrowed from Freddy, the pool attendant down at the Pier House Resort. This implement, if you will, looks like a ten-foot long dentist's tool -- a little nasty saw attached to the end of a long pole. We traded Freddy two framed sunset photos for the use of the Oral-

Saw. We can use it until the next morning at seven a.m. when we have to have it back. At first we had offered Freddy a six-pack of Bud in trade, but Freddy told us that he was a recovering alcoholic.

I've been up on the roof cutting coconuts for two hours. And now it's starting to rain. No worries, a needed, if not well-deserved, break will be good for my mental health.

It continues to rain so Gabrielle makes us a cup of tea (Doris has brought enough Tetleys to last until England wins the World Cup -- or Scotland qualifies). I drink my tea but the rain hasn't stopped, so I decide to take a shower. When I'm done with my shower, and towelling off, I notice that I've left two footprints in the tub. I tell Gabrielle and Doris that if it doesn't stop raining soon, we'll have to break out our brolly and go drink beer. It's what folk do in Key West when it rains, possibly because that's what folk do when it doesn't rain.

I go outside and look at the sky. I've never seen so much water fall from the heavens. And now the wind is picking up. I'm about to scurry back inside, when I spot Mrs Grace beckoning me from the dry confines of her porch.

'Don't forget the berries,' is what she tells me when I get there.

What berries, I ask.

'Those berries in the palm tree you just cut the coconuts out of. What do you suppose they are?'

'Dunno,' I answer. 'I'm out of my element here.'

Mrs Grace smiles maternally in a 'you-poor-dumb-schmuck' manner, then goes on to tell me that the 'berries' are really baby coconuts and if you don't cut them down when you're cutting down the large coconuts, you are going hear about it.

Then she looks at the sky and announces: 'Storm coming. Gonna go batten down the hatches.'

It's still raining, and Doris is reading a book, so Gabrielle and I throw on our yellow foul-weather gear and bike over to the Pineapple Guest House to see if Popcorn Joe wants to go for a beer later. But he's not home. A sign on his backdoor says: GONE TO THE AIRPORT. The rain is so warm, we hang around on the upper deck for a while then leave a message under Popcorn Joe's message.

If possible, the rain has increased and now the streets are flooding. Just a half block away, we spot two guys paddling kayaks. They paddle up William Street from the Historic Seaport and make a left turn on to Caroline Street. Stunned, we watch as they tie up at Pepe's bar and restaurant and wade in for brewskis.

Gabrielle and I have a good laugh over this, then the lightning starts, so we stop laughing and navigate our way back home.

It's now evening and the rain hasn't ceased. It's coming down in sheets. And the lightning is relentless. Mrs Grace was right about the tempest.

I'm worried about Mr Leroy, but I'm sure he's sequestered in the kitchen at the Mobster Lobster with the lads. The storm is getting furious now and the wind is howling. There's nothing else we really can do but pick up a good book and read until it's time for dinner. Gabrielle picks up something by Gerald Seymour and I pick up Lee Weeks. Doris has just finished Ian Rankin and has turned to Carl Hiaasen. Gabrielle and I curl up on our futon, that doubles as our living room couch, open our books and suddenly all the lights go out. I peer out the window and see nothing but blackness.

I go into the kitchen feeling my way along as Audrey Hepburn did in *Wait Until Dark* and find one lonely candle. Our stove is a gas stove, but we've killed the pilot light, remember? I rekindle the pilot light and almost immolate myself in the process. Gabrielle makes us pot of tea. The darkness is bearable if you have a candle and a cuppa.

We hear a knock at the back door and open it and sitting there is Mr Leroy. Then we hear laughter and see Popcorn

Joe, as well. Then we hear even more laughter and we can't believe our eyes, John Rubin steps into view.

'I was at the airport picking John up,' Popcorn Joe tells us. 'I've put him in the efficiency.'

'Rubin! Why didn't you tell us when you were coming?'

'What would you have done, pick me up on your bicycles?'

We laugh some more, then let them all in. Mr Leroy gives Doris a look, then bolts for the bedroom. Gabrielle puts the kettle on.

'Power's out all over the island,' Popcorn Joe tells us. 'There's only one thing you can do in Key West when there's a storm of this magnitude...'

I look at Gabrielle and Doris and Rubin. We are wide-eyed and all ears.

'Seek shelter?' I ask.

'No, go for eats,' Popcorn Joe replies. 'Maybe we can find a restaurant running on a generator.'

I look over at Rubin and he's got the look you get on your face when you are told you need colonic irrigation.

'But the storm, it's deadly out there,' I say.

'Oh, you haven't seen anything yet. Wait for hurricane season. It begins June 1st. It'll make your butt-hole pucker.'

'Your *what* pucker?' Rubin says, and we all burst out laughing.

Popcorn Joe picks up our telephone and starts dialling restaurants.

'Are you open? No? Okay, thanks.'

Then the next one.

'Are you open? No? Thanks.'

It goes on like this for about ten minutes, with the odd 'we're open, but we're closing' then Popcorn Joe strikes gold.

'Are you open? You are? Great. See you in about fifteen.'

Popcorn Joe turns towards us.

'C'mon, I'm treating you guys to dinner.'

Night is night, but with the power out all over the island this is the darkest night we've ever seen. It's eerie driving around Key West, and unnerving. Our headlights cut a tunnel through the ink and passing houses resemble ghost ships bobbing up in view for a moment, then sinking back into a black sea. I'm glad Popcorn Joe is at the helm, and I'm glad it's a four-wheel-drive, high-off-the-ground, monster American truck.

Our goal is to get to a restaurant on Stock Island. We're hoping to dine at a Mexican restaurant called the Cantina. We will have to cross a low bridge to get there. Gabrielle and I are not looking forward to this part of the journey (Doris and Rubin don't know, and we aren't about to mention it). Of even greater concern, we are all secretly praying that the restaurant doesn't run out of alcohol before we get there.

Popcorn Joe's game plan is this: 'Gonna take the beach road, South Roosevelt Boulevard. We'll skirt Smathers Beach, the Key West Airport and Houseboat Row. Should be there in about fifteen.'

But we're not.

Waves are crashing heavily at the beach and eroding the sand. Not good on a small island. Near the airport we can go no farther. The road is flooded and a 30-foot fishing boat has washed up and is blocking our way.

We come about and motor back towards White Street, cleaving six inches of standing water. We will make the approach by going up the spine of the island. I remember RED RIGHT RETURNING, but can't recall if *we* go to the right or we keep the *buoy* to the right. We are the only ones foolish (or thirsty) enough to be out. We have not seen any other living souls. Houses are shut up tight. If there's anyone in there, we sure as hell can't tell.

I look back at Gabrielle and her eyes are as big as, well, coconuts, but she has a smile on her face. Boy, did I marry a game lady.

I glance back at Doris and she has the look you get on your face when you land in Hong Kong for the first time.

I peek over at Rubin and he's biting his fist.

There's a tree down up ahead and we have to manoeuvre around it. I would have said 'swerve to avoid it' but we aren't going fast enough.

Wait! Look! Just up ahead. What's that? We've come to the dreaded bridge. This is the nightmare-from-hell part of this terrifying pursuit of food and foam. Sheets of driving rain are slashing horizontally across the section of pavement we are about to pass over and all sorts of awful images rise unbidden: nasty childhood nightmares associated with black water and vehicles careening out of control and plunging off bridges. As we crawl over the span awash with salt spray, we peer down into the black roiling channel below and I'm concerned about the state of my underwear.

It's nuclear summer with stinging rain and I can't imagine that this restaurant will still be standing, let alone open.

We carry on and I'm sure we've risked our lives for naught.

The 15-minute drive has taken us forty-five minutes.

Then suddenly before us is the gloomy, swimming apparition of the Cantina. The place is black and shuttered. It's closed, damn it! Then lightning strikes and much to our surprise -- and joy -- we see that the car park is absolutely jammed with cars. In fact, it looks as if we're going to have trouble finding a place to park. After two laps around the restaurant, Popcorn Joe mercifully finds refuge in the form of a narrow slot between a rust-bucket '57 Chevy pickup and a late-model Suburu Outback with two kayaks attached to the top (could it be?).

We ride our umbrellas, tiptoes just touching the ground, towards the restaurant's murky main entrance. As the storm tries to fight its way inside, I wrestle with the door so Gabrielle, Doris, Rubin and Popcorn Joe can reach salvation, and we enter a dark, steamy netherworld.

'Resembles the bar in the movie *Star Wars*,' Rubin notes.

Such atmosphere!

An inebriated, giggling hostess -- living *La Vida Loca* -- informs us in heavily accented Cuban-English there is 'Bad News and Worse News.' The bad news is that the restaurant has no power, but we can still order anything that can be cooked on the flame char-broiler -- the worse news is that they have an unlimited supply of slowly warming beer, jugs of cheap red wine and tanks of margaritas.

'So where's the "worse news" in there?' Popcorn Joe asks.

The waitress fixes Joe with scary subtext and says with her floundering accent: 'If the storm worsens, we may all have to spend the night.'

'We speak the same language,' Popcorn Joe responds, and everyone laughs.

Salsa music oozes from the background. A single candle pools a patchy glow on each table. We're led to the last available table, in a deep moody corner. The salsa music seems heavy on the bass here -- or is that the storm? We take our seats and I look around. The lighting may be subdued but the mood is anything but sombre. The bodega is wall-to-wall people. Folk in Key West know how to party! This is *the* place to be on the island (or just off it). This evening will go down in the annals of history as one of the great nights of adventure and romance -- if we survive.

Our colourfully dressed waitress -- who is wearing a bowl of fruit on her head and resembles a young Carmen Miranda -- slips out of the darkness, introduces herself and asks us if we'd like to order drinks. With a straight face Popcorn Joe tells the young *chica* that we are planning on having drinks before drinks and then drinks before dinner. It's clear that Carmen, despite the bowl of fruit on her head, is a carnivore and she fixes Popcorn Joe with a look of 'I would love to jump your bones,' but just says: 'Cool,' and her eyes twinkle with lust.

We order beer and wine, and a pitcher of margaritas and whatever Carmen's drinking. We are going to mix the grape and the grain and we don't care if we get really oiled since there's not going to be anybody else on the road when we drive home. At this rate there may not even be a road.

Suddenly, the wind begins to build even more. It builds and builds and builds and we're sure the roof is going to be ripped off. We're partying hearty and the Second Circle of Hell is just outside the front door. Gabrielle and I look over at Popcorn Joe and he's calmly reading the wine list. He's been here before. A man who's seen it all. The type of guy you want on your side when trouble erupts. A bloke who is indifferent to fear -- and pain.

Our alcohol arrives and we throw it down and order more before the waitress gets sucked back into the black hole that is just beyond our vision.

Damn this is fun.

To heighten the anxiety, Popcorn Joe recounts what it was like to be trapped in Key West in 1992 when hurricane Andrew lay siege to Miami and decimated Homestead and Florida City: 'Andrew was taking dead-aim at Miami, and then during the night it turned slightly to the south. We thought it was going to track right down the Keys. If it had, I wouldn't be sitting here with you right now.'

Lightning and thunder punctuate that last sentence, then Popcorn Joe adds: 'If a hurricane is coming, get out, evacuate. Don't hang around and become a dead romantic.'

I tell Popcorn Joe what Bridget had said, and he just laughs. Then I tell him that I had read somewhere that Key West purportedly could never take a direct hit from a hurricane. Cuba has mountains that rise to over 6,000 feet and any hurricane approaching from the Caribbean and trying to cross Cuba to get to us would be ripped apart by those lofty mountains.

Popcorn Joe says: 'Yeah, I've heard that one, too. Not of a mind to really hang around and test it though.'

Carmen materializes out of the black hole with another pitcher of margaritas. She not only has a nifty sense of fashion, she's clairvoyant. I peer into the subdued lighting surrounding the black hole and focus in on all the other people dining at tables lit only with a candle. What a happy lot. Everyone is chatting in an animated fashion. Enjoying being with whom they are, living life to the fullest. There's no room to be snobbish when you may not see tomorrow.

Every night should be like this!

I'm so taken with the adventure -- and possibly just a bit by the alcohol -- I leap up and shout: '*Après-nous le déluge!*'

But none of the other tables know what I've said, this being insular America.

Then I look over at Rubin and he has taken a cork from one of the wine bottles, stuck it in the flame of the candle and drawn a thick moustache with the charcoal. We all explode with laughter. Rubin just looks deadpan back: 'What?'

Well, the night turned into a night that none of us will forget -- ever. Popcorn Joe and Gabrielle and Doris and Rubin and I talked about everything and nothing. And we made friends with everyone sitting at the neighbouring tables -- once our eyes had adjusted to the dark.

And as hair-raising as it was, no one inside the restaurant wanted the storm to end.

It's the dead middle of the night now and we're all back safe and sound at Villa Alberto. Has that ever happened to you? You suddenly find that you're back in the warm, dry confines of your home -- but you don't have the slightest clue how you got there?

I crawl into bed with Gabrielle. There's still no power and it's sultry and we can hear the rain pelting the tin roof of our home. The storm rages on, but somehow it's not so alarming now. I say 'I'm glad Doris is here. She's always game for anything.' And Gabrielle says 'I love you' and I say 'I love you' back. And then we have a good laugh, you see, we hear tiny, almost inaudible little snores.

No, it's not Doris.

Mr Leroy is in here with us.

CHAPTER 11

And then came the heat.

And Doris scarpered.

The lazy days of summer were suddenly upon us and an oppressive sauna-like atmosphere lay upon the island and sucked the energy from every living creature during the middle of the day. If we wished to maintain our sterling level of renovations around Villa Alberto, we would have to get up early in the morning, when it was cool, or wait until we returned home from Mallory Square in the evening, when it was dark.

A leak had sprung in our roof, so to beat the heat, I had to climb up there just after sunrise. Even this time of the morning it can be inhumanly humid in Key West, especially when the overnight temperature has not dipped below 82 degrees Fahrenheit. We were living in air conditioning now, and when we opened our back door, even at the ungodly crack of dawn, it felt as if someone had slapped us in the face with a steaming Turkish towel.

Just so you know, I don't have any experience fixing roofs, Mr Tosser wasn't going to have it done for us, so I had to try to figure out how to do it on my own. The leak was right over our bed, but when I went up on the gigantic sun reflector that was our tin roof and patched the entire area above the bed, we still had a leak. The source of the leak was elsewhere, but I didn't know that, did I? Eventually, Popcorn Joe popped by and enlightened me to the exotic vagaries of roof leakage and showed me how the source of an offending leak could be great distances away from where the Chinese water torture was taking place.

* * *

Popcorn Joe has given us his old computer. It's from the Jurassic period. The screen is the size of an oscilloscope, but we don't mind. We use the computer to access the Internet, and we read all there is about remodelling and renovating. And Chinese water torture.

Gabrielle and Mr Leroy are tiling the bathroom floor. Gabrielle is in doing the hands-on dirty work. Mr Leroy is sitting in the sink, supervising. Our bathroom, which we thought was rectangular, is apparently trapezoidal. This we didn't discover until Gabrielle tried to fit the last pieces of the tiling puzzle into place. It's always this way, isn't it? Houses are not symmetrical. Houses are not plumb. Did you ever try to get that last sheet of wallpaper with the vertical stripes to match up? Or the carpet to fit the corner? Or the door hung so that it actually closed? And then opened again? Without using the Jaws of Life?

I'm out on the back deck destroying tile. I'm meant to be out here *splitting* the remaining pieces of tile into the correct geometric angles, so that Gabrielle can finish the puzzle. I am nothing without the proper tools. Let alone skills.

Mr Leroy has decided to knock off for the rest of the afternoon and has positioned himself in the middle of our bed -- on his back. He's meant to be at the Mobster-Lobster by 7 p.m. to work the dinner crowd. So I let him sleep. He has a long night ahead.

Through sheer determination (and the dangling carrot of margaritas) Gabrielle has managed to finish tiling the bathroom. The floor is so dazzlingly white and pristine, it now makes the tub appear dull and dingy. Undaunted, we pedal out to K-Mart and purchase a tropical shower curtain with palm trees on it to hide the tub that I have spent hours scouring.

* * *

It's hot today. Withering hot. We don't have to work at the Pineapple Guest House, so we hop on our bikes and pedal five minutes over to the beach at Ft. Zack. The only way to survive the crushing heat of the Key West summer is to spend the afternoon underwater.

At the beach we find the sea calm, as glassy and clear as the water in the St. Ives harbour. We've brought our snorkels and masks, so we spend the afternoon peering at all the undersea creatures who are spending their afternoon peering back at us. I sneeze underwater and make Gabrielle laugh and she has to surface.

We've brought an enormous watermelon for lunch, so we filet the beast, sit in the shade under a palm tree that resembles our shower curtain and feast. For some reason the watermelon tastes better out here at the beach than it does back home in the A/C. When we finish we get right back in the water so we will be in time for the cramps. We put our masks back on and explore the ocean floor. We are in three feet of water. A large school of the marine equivalent of lemmings swims with us and when I reach out a hand the entire shimmering school magically shifts just out of reach in a Bolshoi-esque choreographed fishy fashion.

The undersea world brings out childlike wonder.

We splash out of the sea and cross the burning sand to the shade under our palm tree. We dig into some more watermelon and I have a peep at my wife who is thoroughly enjoying every minute of the day. I'm surprised to note that Gabrielle's auburn hair is bleaching from the salt and the sun and I'm now married to a blonde. We look healthier and feel healthier, and we are deliriously happy here in paradise.

* * *

And old friend (well, he's not old, but you get what I mean) Johnny Beerling has come to visit. He's travelling around the Caribbean for six weeks, hitting Jamaica and Cuba, then over to New Orleans and Key West, all the while lecturing on cruise liners about his illustrious 36-year career at the BBC. 'It's a hard life but someone has to do it!' he tells us.

Having been the 'heart and soul' of Radio 1, Johnny's written the definitive book entitled: **RADIO 1, The Inside Scene**. Gabrielle grew up listening to many of the DJs such as Noel Edmonds, Johnnie Walker and Tony Blackburn, so we are eager to read the book.

Beerling has a short layover in Key West, and it's scorching, so we are motoring up to Bahia Honda State Park to go snorkelling. And then later in the evening, if we don't go fishing off Mallory Pier for tarpon, we will ply Johnny with mojitos and get him to recount some of his great stories. Being a dyed-in-the-wool, I mean, dyed-in-the-tie-dye Beatles' fan, I, for one, want to know all about the 14-hour production he did about the Fab Four.

To get to this point, it may take numerous mojitos.

* * *

In the summers, Popcorn Joe goes on holiday for a month or two to beat the heat, get off the island and, I presume, escape the world of popcorn for a while. Popcorn Joe liked to holiday in Wyoming where he could mountain bike. This was his passion. And his favourite town was a sleepy hamlet of seventy-five inhabitants called Red Rock. When Popcorn Joe first told us about the place I had asked him what the population was.

'It's seventy five,' Joe said.

'Seventy-five hundred?' I asked.

'No, seventy five,' Joe said.

'Seventy-five thousand?' Gabrielle asked.

'No,' Joe said, laughing. 'Just seventy-five!'

From that day on Gabrielle and I had our own code/dialect with Popcorn Joe. If we saw him down at Mallory or tooling around the island on his moped or zooming along the promenade at the beach on his rollerblades, we would shout out: 'Seventy-five thousand?' And Joe would yell back: 'No, just seventy five!'

When the day came for Popcorn Joe to begin his long awaited holiday, Gabrielle and I left Villa Alberto early and went over to Joe's for our traditional kick-your-arse Cuban coffee. We were to be in charge of the Pineapple Guest House while Joe pursued mountain-bike nirvana by day (and toured nearby meat markets by night), so Popcorn Joe gave us last-minute instructions, which essentially amounted to: 'If anybody dies in one of the apartments while I'm gone, don't try to get a hold of me, they'll still be dead when I get back.'

And then we drove Popcorn Joe to the airport in the truck. He was outfitted in tan slacks (we had never seen Popcorn Joe in anything other than shorts), loafers, no socks and a tan cotton jacket that just covered a T-shirt, which read: 'Free Moustache Rides'.

Over the course of the next few weeks, Gabrielle and I continued with the remodelling of Villa Alberto: We painted the entire exterior, painted more rooms inside, patched holes where there shouldn't have been holes, trimmed the jungle out back and pruned the floral boscage up front. We installed a lock the size of your fist on the gate that led into the backyard/jungle so no one would steal our new/used bikes. And we spread yards of gravel in our driveway even though we didn't own anything that we could park there. We even built a little table so we could eat out on our back deck on the warm evenings and test the effectiveness of *OFF!*

With Popcorn Joe gone walkabout, Gabrielle and I soon developed a daily routine: Renovate Villa Alberto at the crack of waking up, see to chores at the guest house until noon, remain submerged in the Atlantic Ocean until four, sell sunset photos down at Mallory until nine (we are now flogging large prints mounted under glass in funky driftwood-esque frames), then back over to the guest house to make sure it was still standing -- and collapse.

As the days of summer slipped by and the heat built, the guest house at night became a balmy tranquil oasis. All the tenants were over on Duval Street drinking pubs dry and raising hell, and with popcorn Joe gone, there was no one up on his back deck and his apartment was all locked up and dark. And it was wonderful to sit out under the stars and watch the meteor showers or just listen to the gentle breezes in the palm trees and sip a cool tropical, rum-laced drink. It was a peaceful time in our less than stressful schedule, and we revelled in the serenity and enjoyed immensely each and every day.

But then one night our peaceful existence changed.

We stopped by the guest house, climbed up the stairs to the back deck and found the entire kitchen door of Popcorn Joe's apartment crushed in. Someone had broken into the Pineapple Guest House on our watch!

While we were down at Mallory and all the guests were either out or passed out, someone had climbed the back outside stairs and broken through Popcorn Joe's kitchen door. I don't mean they 'broke in', they 'broke through'. The door had had glass panels from top to bottom and some twisted smack-head had shattered the entire door and left a great splintered gaping toothy maw.

You can imagine our horror. And how awful we felt. And how frightened we were. I've always been one who is fearless, until something happens, of course.

We ran into Popcorn Joe's office and the receipts for the week had been stolen. Why hadn't we gone to the bank and made a deposit instead of depositing ourselves at the beach?

'Go grab the machete. He might still be around.'

I grabbed the machete and Gabrielle grabbed a baseball bat and we went room to room in Joe's flat looking for the burglar. Then we tentatively climbed the stairs up to our old attic and searched there, as well.

No one.

'We'd better ring the police.'

'We can't. What if they ask if we have work permits?'

'Joe will sack us if we don't report it. He'll think it was us.'

'What if the police ask us what we're doing here?'

'We'll just say we're looking after the place while Joe's gone.'

'Hope they don't recognise me.'

'Crap.'

We telephoned the police and the police came right away. They searched the house and our old attic upstairs all over again. And we filled out a police report. The police left without recognizing me or asking us any questions. And then we felt even more awful. And what was worse, we felt incompetent. It was all our fault. It was dereliction of duty.

'Should we call Popcorn Joe and tell him what happened?' I asked Gabrielle.

'No, remember what he said?'

'Yeah, but it seems much worse now that something's happened.'

'You're right. But we still can't call.'

'I think I got to call. I feel awful.'

'And that's why we can't. Joe doesn't want to feel awful. We can't call.'

So we didn't, instead we took a couple of large sheets of plywood, meant for hurricane season, and boarded up the imploded hole where the kitchen door had once lived. Then we called Don and Shirley. Don was a master at building anything and everything, and the next day he and Shirley kindly came over and installed a kitchen door that was a replica of the old one. We painted it and it looked as good as new. And then we drank an intemperate amount of alcohol and wondered if Popcorn Joe was going to sack us when he returned.

* * *

There's a new 'entertainer' at Mallory Square. He's the Bird-Man. He has a parrot. A green-wing Macaw. Just so you know, this is a big bird. And it's aggressive. But that's not the bad part. The Bird-Man has set up across from our sunset photo display. We're trying to sell sunset photos and there's a rapacious pterodactyl screeching and snapping at anyone who comes within 20 feet of our pitch. And that's not the bad part, either. The Bird-Man has just tossed his pterodactyl into the air in an attempt to impress the crowd with clipped-wing flight and the great hollow-boned raptor has stalled on takeoff and flown smack into our display causing it to crash, yes, in so many shattered pieces, to the ground -- glass-framed prints included.

Our display now resembles Popcorn Joe's kitchen door just after the break-in, only we have much more broken glass -- and an unconscious green-wing Macaw.

Things couldn't get any worse for us.

Or could they?

Popcorn Joe returns home tomorrow.

CHAPTER 12

Popcorn Joe flew into Key West in the middle of a late-summer meteorological fiesta. The temperature was a volatile 33 degrees Celsius, the skies were angry and our moods were partly cloudy. We were looking forward to having our friend back, but we were dreading telling him about the break-in.

When we arrived at the airport we were informed by an airline employee, a Parrot Head, that Popcorn Joe's airplane was 'experiencing a delay'. An evil storm had passed through Miami and apparently a tornado had skipped across Biscayne Bay towards downtown and had scared the living shit out of everyone in the high rises who could afford a good view.

Gabrielle and I sheltered in Arrivals/Departures, sardined with nervous travelling folk of questionable hygiene and stared gloomily out at a sky that was deteriorating, and fast. Suddenly, and with great drama might I add, there was a clap of thunder and a commuter aircraft dropped wailing out of the pregnant sky, banked once, came in hot and set down on the 4,800 foot runway with a silent puff of smoke from its tires. The 'puddle-jumper' fishtailed wildly and eventually lurched to an unscheduled stop just short of the salt ponds. If an airplane could ever look frightened, then this was the one.

The tropical summer gods had chased it whimpering from the sky.

(FYI: The short length of Key West's runway prohibits the handful of regional jets from filling up with passengers (and fuel) on the hottest and most humid days of the year. Balmy weather affects the planes' performance negatively and makes the added weight a risk. This little titbit fails to get a mention in the in-flight magazines.)

Nothing ever fazed Popcorn Joe, and he was his cheery, laid-back self as he calmly deplaned. That could not be said for the rest of the rubber-legged passengers who all appeared overly rich in chlorophyll (their colour did not return until they rose from genuflecting and kissing Mother Earth).

'I could murder a beer!' Popcorn Joe announced, as he hugged Gabrielle and slapped me about in that pseudo-macho American way.

Beer! What luck! I thought. Gabrielle and I had conspired to ply Popcorn Joe with buckets of alcohol and give him the bad news about the break-in when he was in a semi-comatose state and could no longer input details.

Once we reached the car park, Popcorn Joe bellowed: 'You drive, Jon! I wanna take in the sights. It's great to be home!'

'Where do you want to go?' Gabrielle asked, as all three of us squeezed into the front seat of the pickup truck.

'You choose,' Popcorn Joe said ebulliently.

We motored down South Roosevelt Boulevard and about the time we hit Higgs Beach the weather took a turn for the worse. Not easy on a day where it had already gone downhill about as far as it could go.

We entered the Old Town leaving a foamy wake behind in the flooded street and as a surprise we took Popcorn Joe to a moody bar with serious charm on the corner of Petronia and Duval.

'Ever been here?' I asked.

Popcorn Joe looked around, formed a funny look on his face and said: 'Can't say that I have, amigo, but then who am I to judge people? Let's drink!'

We were worried that Popcorn Joe wouldn't like the venue, but then Gabrielle reminded me that we could feel secure in the knowledge that any haunt that served cold beer was just fine with Joe. That was his only requirement. He was an easy guy to please.

I ordered a margarita for Gabrielle and a pitcher of beer for the Popcorn man and me. When the lifesaving drinks arrived, we toasted Joe's return, began the unending process of the quenching of thirst and watched the rain cascade down the tin roofs across Duval Street.

Suddenly, Popcorn Joe asked: 'So how did it go while I was gone?'

I heard a small scream come from Gabrielle.

'How did what go while you were gone?' I said.

'How'd things go at the guest house? I want to hear all about it.'

'Oh, there's so much to report,' I began, 'but there's plenty of time to do all that. But first, we want to know how your holiday was.'

'Tell. Tell,' Gabrielle said.

So Popcorn Joe spent the next hour recounting his trip to the Wild Wild West and how much he rode his mountain bike and how he saw a buffalo and how he got laid, frequently (not by the buffalo). We ordered another margarita and another pitcher of beer, and then Popcorn Joe said, a bit too eagerly: 'So, how did it go while I was gone?'

I eyed Gabrielle and she screamed: 'Look!'

A gaggle of well-sozzled revellers was assembled by the front window. They were holding up signs with numbers on them as Olympic judges do. Any and all young males were the target and everyone in the bar would cheer when one of the passing males received a high score. One unsuspecting lad, with a weightlifter's body and sporting Glasgow Rangers' strips, received a perfect 10 and the bar went wild. Apparently the lad was unimpressed with his results as he responded digitally.

'So how did it go while I was away?'

Gabrielle and I were grasping for straws and sinking fast, so I flagged down the cocktail waitress -- who had legs up to here -- and ordered two Alabama Slammers, one for Gabrielle and me, and a Screaming Orgasm for Popcorn Joe (even though he probably had been the recipient of plenty of those on holiday).

We threw our shots back.

'So tell me already!' Joe said.

'We can't!' Gabrielle blurted.

'Why not?' Joe asked.

'Why not?' I repeated. Even I was curious.

'Because, I, ah, have to go to the loo.'

When Gabrielle returned, she was carrying a tray of three shots of wicked schnapps that smelled not unlike acetone.

'Down the hatch!'

We threw the acetone down. Suddenly, Popcorn Joe began laughing. Gabrielle and I shot each other a look. It was contagious. We began laughing as people do for no reason when alcohol is the governing body. And then Popcorn Joe really began to laugh and he said: 'I know all about the break-in. For crissakes, your faces have been slaying me. Got friends on the police force, remember? I've known all about that doo-dah for the last two weeks.'

Then Joe became very serious: 'There is something that I don't know, though.'

'What?' Gabrielle asked, eyeing me.

'Why in the hell did you bring me to this gay bar?'

Gabrielle and I looked about. It was now dark out. The rain had ceased. The moon was peeking from behind a palm tree. The temperature had plummeted to a balmy 78 degrees. Ceiling fans were circling lazily overhead. The Olympic judges, now shirtless, were dancing in a dark corner. We were drinking in a radiantly gay bar.

And we still had our jobs.

Life was good.

Positively grand.

Gabrielle and I looked over at Joe, and he was just smiling back. 'How 'bout a couple for the road?'

'Why not!' I said. 'If we still have time.'

The cocktail waitress (with the legs up to here) was loping by so I enquired as to when the joint closed.

'Four a.m.,' came a husky reply.

We all did a double-take.

No.

Couldn't be.

Could it?

* * *

Gabrielle's sister, Alicyn, and her husband, Mike, have just arrived. At this rate we will run out of friends and family in the UK who haven't visited us -- in about ten years.

Alicyn and Mike have a farm in Perthshire. It's where I woke up after experiencing/surviving my first hogmanay. I was meant to be the designated driver, but I ended up being the designated drinker.

Mike is a voracious reader and he spends his days on our deck, in the shade, devouring books. He wants to read this one when I've finished, so that's why I'm giving them a mention. Alicyn and Mike don't know they are in here.

America is an eye-opener for Mike and Alicyn. They can't believe how inexpensive petrol is. Or how bartenders don't fill a glass of beer to the top. Or how cold the beer is.

* * *

We've purchased a hammock. And we've strung it between the two palm trees in our backyard. The hammock holds both of us. Three, if you count Mr Leroy. When we are not renovating Villa Alberto, we are lying in the hammock admiring our work.

Gabrielle and Alicyn have taken all the coconuts that have fallen and placed them -- as if they were stones from the field -- around our garden out back.

And they've taken root.

We didn't know this would happen.

And now we have 54 baby palm trees growing in our backyard.

On top of that, Gabrielle and Alicyn have been fertilizing the plumeria tree out front and it is a glorious picture of pastel pinks and searing magentas. Its fragrance is so piercing, we can smell its sweet perfume when we enter the lane late at night. It has brought us great joy.

Villa Alberto is finally taking shape. It no longer resembles a derelict barracks, rather a bright, cheerful cottage. We are the envy of the lane. Mrs Grace, Taxi-Man, Pig-Man, all our dear neighbours (except the Bitch-Bovine) have bestowed compliments. Even a corpulent stranger, a local estate agent, has stopped by and congratulated us on our effort.

The heat is now debilitating. Sure, there are hotter places on the planet, but the combination of the humidity and curious lack of trade winds is taking its toll.

So we live in the hammock. Sometimes we read. Sometimes we snooze. Sometimes we read a bad book, and that puts us to sleep. And we don't feel guilty. Not in this heat. Whoever invented the siesta, we would like to thank.

* * *

We strolled down to the marina by the Ocean Key Resort to watch the fishing boats return. This is a form of entertainment in Key West. When the first boats arrive everyone crowds around wide-eyed and with great expectation as sunburnt crew with raccoon eyes unload a cross section of coveted gulf-stream game fish and fling them unceremoniously up on to the quay. While the captain of the charter boat holds sway, books charters for the next day and pops open a can of beer, the first mate filets the day's catch with surgeon-like skill so that you, the great sportsman, may have your wife cook it up back at your self-catering flat. You tell your wife how much money you will save by not having to take her and the kids to dinner. Not only does your wife see through this ruse (the charter boat set you back $400 for the day), but she really wanted to go out to dinner in the first place so that she didn't have to cook, you see, SHE'S ON HOLIDAY, TOO!

When the charter boats return, they fly a flag to show the world that they've landed a marlin or sailfish or Jaws, but frequently when you run up to the boat to behold the great beasts being unloaded, you find nothing. In the spirit of conservation, 'catch and release' is the politically correct game in town. You may struggle with a marlin or a bull dolphin (no relation to Flipper), but instead of taking its life, you release it so it can live another day.

And be caught another day.

And released another day.

Gabrielle and I were about to bolt for the Bull when we spotted one last fishing boat chug up the channel and hang a starboard into the harbour. Being the curious creatures that we are we went over to investigate. This boat not only had the flag flying, it also had the beast: A fairly impressive member of the shark family. Wow! Were we ever the lucky ones.

The first mate held open the mouth for all of us to see the numerous rows of menacing razor-sharp teeth -- then let the jaws snap shut again. The sight of this would put you right off snorkelling (or possibly dating anyone with an overbite).

'Are you going to filet it?' I asked, now au fait to quay-side jargon.

'No, gonna take it home to bed with me,' the skipper said, then shook his head in a what-a-dumb-fucking-question manner.

At my expense, everyone laughed.

We left the tainted ambiance of the charter boats behind and took a walk up Whitehead Street. Just after we passed

Greene Street, we heard a woman screaming absolute bloody murder. A domestic? We didn't know what to do. Call the cops? Go see what was happening? Run? About now a bin man, of Bahamian descent, who was picking up rubbish at a neighbouring guest house, came sprinting up and tore around the back of the house. There's safety in numbers, so we followed. In the backyard, a seriously frightened woman was standing there frozen in place by a seven-foot black snake that had its head raised a few feet off the ground. Gabrielle and I took a step back. The bloody thing looked like a cobra.

'Rat snake!' shouted the intrepid bin man and, on that, he reached down and deftly grabbed the non-venomous snake by the back of its scaly head.

'Get it out of here!' pleaded the woman.

'I'll second that!' Gabrielle chimed in.

'I'll take care of it, ma'am,' said the bin man.

My God, this bloke was the type of guy you wanted to get to know. Gabrielle and I followed as our new hero strolled to his truck with the snake now dangling down to the ground, climbed in, stuck his hand out the window with the enormous black reptile now coiling around his forearm and drove off down Whitehead Street.

Bin men in paradise go the extra mile.

We headed up Whitehead Street to Kelly's on the corner of Caroline. There's fantastic atmosphere here, indoors and out. This is where you want to be kicking back on a warm summer evening. And you want to get your snappers into a piece of Key Lime pie, the official and celebrated pie of Key West and the Florida Keys. One should not go through life without sampling this regional delight.

There are loads of books and Pan Am memorabilia in Kelly's and we were reading about Pan Am's first flight from Key West to Havana in 1927 (took one hour and ten minutes to fly 90 miles), when Gabrielle suddenly froze and pointed at a rusted-out Ford pickup motoring by. In the back bed, a seven-foot shark was sticking out. At the helm was Captain

Comedian. We couldn't believe our eyes, he was taking the shark home with him.

'A candlelit dinner, a little white wine -- goes well with fish -- some romantic music, talk of commitment...' Gabrielle said, and we had a good laugh.

* * *

We are being invaded by scorpions. Suddenly, they are everywhere. They live underground and the warm summer rains bring them out. Despite being nocturnal, we see them early in the morning, in the heat of the day and just before bedtime. They are never far away. And they respect no man's privacy.

My first encounter with a scorpion was early one steamy morning when I popped into the corner market -- a little Mom & Pop establishment -- run by a lesbian couple. Three macho-macho construction workers and I were standing at the espresso machine waiting to order café *con leche* when a black scorpion crawled out from beneath the salt & vinegar Pringles display. Well, you've never heard such screams -- and they were coming from the construction workers. As all of us danced like the Rutland Morris Men to get out of the way, the petite (albeit butch) owner of the market flew from behind the counter and squashed the scorpion with, get ready, her bare foot. Then she gave the three burly construction workers, who had formed a scrum in a corner, an amused look and said: 'It's all over now, ladies.'

She probably would have blown an insult my way, as well, but I don't think she noticed me hiding behind the Chewing Tobacco display.

On another occasion, Gabrielle and I were getting ready to go to sleep. I had just tucked Mr Leroy in down by Gabrielle's feet and was leaning over to turn out the light on our bedside orange crate when I saw a rather impressive black specimen crawling across the wall right above my pillow. You can see our dilemma, can't you? Was he a lone interloper or did he come with friends? If one gained entry, a whole fraternity could have made the trip.

In a display of courage to my wife, I captured the bugger with a pint glass I had purloined from Finnegan's Wake on Grinnell Street. Then Gabrielle and I stripped the bed, rotated the mattress and looked behind and under everything in the house, twice.

Mr Leroy was the only one who slept well that night.

A lot of homes in Key West have hardwood floors (remember the Classifieds?). Hardwood is cooler than carpet and a much better all-around deal when it comes to a muggy, sandy, flea-infested island. One night (cue the music from your favourite horror flick soundtrack), Gabrielle was encamped on the cool hardwood floor with a glass of Shiraz and an impressive plate of nachos, I was on the futon. We were watching the start of a less-than-diverting 'B' horror film, *Attack of the Killer Tomatoes*, when Gabrielle suddenly hit the 'mute' button on our gizmo (this had no impact on the movie's exposition, by the way), and said: 'Did you hear that?'

We listened together. Nothing. Listened some more. Still nothing. Listened one last time and then we heard it. The most evil hair-raising sound a person could ever want to hear: small arachnid feet on a well-varnished hardwood floor, CLICK, CLACK. CLICK, CLACK. Strolling out of our bedroom was a large, noisy arthropod, stinger curled forward in a menacing arc.

CLICK, CLACK. CLICK, CLACK. Gabrielle jumped up on the couch with me, and we hugged each other as little old ladies do when they've seen a mouse. Then, remembering that I was the man of the house, I sprang into action and tried to club the shit out of the scorpion with my sand wedge. Of course, I missed him completely because I can't hit anything with a sand wedge. But all was not lost, Gabrielle had read on the oscilloscope that scorpions have really bad eyesight -- so he wasn't there to enjoy the movie -- and all she had to do was open the front door and the little blighter tumbled blindly outside and landed in front of the plumeria tree.

When all the excitement died down, we turned our attention back to the movie where America was facing a crisis of epic proportions: Murderous, humongous, mutant tomatoes were on the rampage and they were indiscriminately killing innocent people in cities from coast to coast!

And suddenly one noisy little scorpion with bad eyesight didn't seem quite so threatening.

CHAPTER 13

The first thing we do when we get up in the morning -- other than drag Mr Leroy kicking and screaming off the bed and let him out -- is turn on the Weather Channel. Every eight minutes they have local weather. Insightfully enough, it's called LOCAL ON THE 8s. Then at fifty minutes past the hour they give us the TROPICAL UPDATE. The Tropical Update, among other things, alerts us to any tropical development in the Atlantic basin and the Gulf of Mexico.

We pay special attention to everything the Weather Channel says. We monitor all updates. We note every forecast. Then we ignore it all. None of the weather prognoses end up being accurate anyway.

Today's forecast was for an 80-per-cent chance of rain. It's now almost midnight and we haven't had a drop of precipitation all day, just cloudless skies and endless scorching sunshine.

Yesterday, there was a 20-per-cent chance of rain and it pissed like a racehorse from morning till night.

Tomorrow, there's a 50-per-cent chance of rain, so we don't have the faintest idea what's in store for us. Perhaps an eclipse of the sun.

Or a near miss from an asteroid.

Or a rogue tsunami.

No one knows for sure.

For reasons which I can't fathom, the weather folk are able to get the tides right, so I guess that's something. They said high tide would occur at exactly eleven-ten a.m. So we went and looked and there it was! High tide and everything. Right on time. We were so impressed and the water was so inviting we decided to go in for a little swim, but then it started to rain.

I really don't understand any of it at all.

Remember me telling you that the heat had set in? Do you remember that? Well, I must have lied, because somehow it seems even hotter. Stickier. Steamier. Sweatier. More suffocating. Super prickly heat.

The temperature of the ocean is now 28 degrees (I've had showers that weren't that warm). The moisture rises off the warm surface of the sea, makes the atmosphere a soggy steaming sponge and forms clouds, gigantic towering anvil-shaped thunderheads. And then blinding shards of lightning streak from the sky (the weather swots swear it goes from the earth, up, and they ought to know) and we get bombarded with the most hellacious thunder. The thunder sounds different down here at the edge of the tropics. More reverberating. More booming. Something has really pissed-off the gods -- possibly the weather swots.

Watching the Weather Channel has ceased to be a source of information for us. Now, it is a source of amusement.

And so is the local radio's Lost & Found pet spot. It's fondly called the PET PATROL, and it's wacky, quirky and a downright hoot. Here's an example of some creatures down on their luck. 'Lost: large iguana. "Banjo" is green with sort of a Mohawk. He needs his medication or he becomes aggressive...' Or 'Lost: free-range chicken. Goes by the name of "Dickie". Dickie is a cock...'

'How can he be lost if he's "free-range"?' my wife asks me. Or 'Lost: large black rat snake. Looks like a cobra...' Hey!

Gabrielle and I have been listening to this same spot for ten days straight now. We don't go out after dark much anymore.

$$* \quad * \quad *$$

A squall line thundered through early this morning and dropped an eye-popping amount of rain and woke us up before it was light. If you've never been ripped from your addled dreams in the wee hours by 'frog-strangling' rains and crashing thunder, you have missed one of nature's little jokes. Once your pulse drops back below the boiling point, and you've changed your knickers, it's all quite diverting.

The rain moved offshore, but the lightning continued, so Gabrielle grabbed Mr Leroy and we ran out back and crawled up into the hammock and watched the light show. Nothing ever fazes Mr Leroy, but even he seemed impressed by the heavenly pyrotechnics. The air was already heavy and unbearable and it was charged with power and violence, as if it were going to explode.

When the light show ended we went back inside and I made some coffee, not that we needed the caffeine, mind you, not after the gods' percussion-section solo. I took two steaming cups into the living room where Gabrielle and Mr Leroy were perched on the edge of the futon watching, yes you've guessed it, the Weather Channel.

'Check it out,' Gabrielle said.

Something called a 'Tropical Wave' had rolled off the African Coast, well south of the Canaries, and was now moving westward through an enchantingly mysterious part of the world known as the Intertropical Convergence Zone.

(FYI: The Intertropical Convergence Zone, also known also as the doldrums, is the region that encircles the earth, near the equator, where the trade winds of the Northern and Southern Hemispheres collide. The intense sun and warm water of the equator heat the air in the Intertropical Convergence Zone, raising its humidity and causing it to rise. As the air rises it cools, releasing the accumulated moisture in an almost perpetual parade of thunderstorms, which then march relentlessly from Africa towards the Caribbean, Cuba and eventually Florida.)

We watched with eyes glued to the tube as an all too familiar face at the Weather Channel said something about 'significant in size' and 'this bears watching'.

'What does this all mean?' Gabrielle asked.

'Who in the hell knows anymore,' I said. 'I'm going to go buy a newspaper.'

Key West before dawn is a ghost town, a muggy, heady ghost town, devoid of human life, except for the odd wino passed out in the bushes, of course.

This morning, possibly on account of all the rain and lightning, the island seemed surreally dead. Even the winos weren't sleeping it off, al fresco.

I shuffled down Whitehead Street until I reached the Green Parrot (which bore the usual scars from the previous night's debauchery), and turned right on to Southard. Halfway down the block and across the street, a Doberman slabbered at me from behind a chain-linked fence. Someone's watchdog, I surmised, and an effective one at that. The Doberman barked threateningly at me in that I-want-to-rip-your-throat-out way that Nazi dogs sometimes do, so I gave him the finger and hurried farther down the street and there on the murky corner of Southard and Duval, under a broken street lamp, was my *Open All Hours* vending machine selling the Mullet Wrap. I threw two quarters into the little slot, opened the door (it almost took my arm off), pulled out a middle copy from the pile and turned around.

Standing there, eyeing me with sincere malice, was the Doberman. How did he get out? Did he have his own key? Apparently, I had made a bad impression when I flipped him off.

I peered up Duval Street. Then down Duval Street. The streets were black and wet and shiny from the rain, and deserted. I turned and glanced back at the Doberman, hoping he had magically disappeared, but he hadn't. He was still there. And now he had a friend. An enormous matted-hair lurcher.

'Nice doggies,' I whimpered, and they both showed me their teeth.

I was dead-meat. What was I going to do? What would you have done?

At times like this, I always cast my mind back to the Discovery Channel and do a quick 'search' of all past shows I've watched -- and where I've screamed 'run little one, run!' -- as some hell-bent carnivorous eating-machine bounded, smacking its snappers, after a defenceless miniature dik-dik.

And regarding humans, as lunch, the Discovery Channel always advises to 'establish dominance', so in my best stage voice I yelled: 'Fuck off ye mangy beasts!'

And do you know how these two hormonal hounds responded to my macho outburst? They bared their teeth again and then lunged at me. Barking and snapping and drooling and dripping. How rude! I faltered back into the doorway of a darkened business and in desperation tried the door, but no go. And then do you know what? When I turned back, there were five slavering hounds. All the howls and yowls had attracted every other flesh-eating feral canine on the island and suddenly I was surrounded by what resembled a pack of frothing-at-the-mouth, rife-with-rabies wolves with glistening fangs and evil, yellow eyes.

And let me tell you right up front, I was scared. I would have shit my pants had I not already done that on account of the aforementioned explosive thunder. Awful things can happen in far-flung parts of the world and down here 90 miles from Havana I was about as far-flung as a person needed to be to find trouble.

The pack snarled savagely and I stared into those carnivorous eyes and saw primal instincts -- and from time to time my own terrified image. On any other morning there might have been someone else up and about, but not this rainy, blackened, primordial morning from hell.

Then for some inexplicable reason my own instincts took over. Just when the yapping brutes were licking their chops and closing in for the dismemberment, I did something that almost everyone of us has done at one time or another, I rolled up my newspaper and waved it at them and yelled Bad dog! and they all backed off in one great wave of matted fur, tails tucked beneath their scrawny legs.

I blew out my cheeks and walked casually home, only looking over my shoulder about a hundred times, and when I arrived at Villa Alberto, Gabrielle had another cup of coffee waiting for me, and I told her all about my brush with death-by-dog and then we discussed the pros and cons of subscribing to the Mullet Wrap, so I wouldn't have to venture out.

And decided against it.

* * *

The temperature of the ocean has climbed to 30 degrees. The water is now so warm, we have to get out to cool off. I am not exaggerating this. After snorkelling today, we purchased ice creams, but they suffered nuclear meltdown before we were halfway down to the good bits and they dripped all over us. To wash off, we went back in the ocean. Then we had to get out again to cool off.

Summer is dragging and the heat is relentless. We don't think autumn will ever come to this part of the world. Gabrielle says we will probably just hit spring and then jump right back into summer. Business at Mallory has died a quick death and the guest house is vacant. We're not bringing in any money and now the flagrantly odious Mr Tosser has raised our rent. We complained, and he told us 'If you don't like it, move'.

Mr Tosser wants a good slapping.

In the evenings we go down to the pier, set up our photographic display, watch the glorious sunsets with the other starving vendors and performers, then tear down our display and go home, penniless. We are told that business will pick up for Fantasy Fest -- in October. Which is autumn. But bleeding autumn isn't coming, is it?

* * *

Our toilet backed up this morning -- into our bathtub. This is not how we had planned to start the day, but it beats the hell out of death-by-Doberman. Plumbing is an unparalleled mystery to me. How can you flush your toilet and end up with high tide in the tub?

I grabbed the plunger and plunged the toilet, and the effluence swirled higher in the tub. Then I plunged the tub and the raw sewage mysteriously disappeared. So I cleaned the tub with a cocktail of bleach and abrasives. Then we took a shower and the toilet backed up. Then I flushed the toilet and we had a tub full again.

'Let's go tell our landlord,' Gabrielle said.

'I refuse to go see Mr Tosser. Every time we go there he treats us like sewage and he ruins our day. We didn't come to Key West to have our day ruined by a bum-fuck like that sorry sack of shit!'

I looked over at my wife and she had taken a step back, such was my deportment. 'Sorry,' I said. 'I'm a bit wound up.'

'You're an alarm clock.'

'The guy makes my blood boil.'

'I'll go on my own.'

'I would never let you do that. I'm coming.'

We bicycled over to Mr Tosser's office and found him sitting with his feet up on his desk again. Gabrielle purposely wore a T-shirt that said: I'M TRYING TO IMAGINE YOU WITH A PERSONALITY. We told Mr Tosser about our toilet and we told him about our shower. And do you know what this multimillionaire piece-of-shit said to us? 'So shower at the beach.'

Gabrielle gave the prick a look that the Doberman had given me and I thought she was going to go for his carotid.

'Can't you just call the plumber?' I asked.

And *then* do you know what this dick-breath said? 'Listen, I'm really busy right now. Come back on Monday.'

'But it's Friday,' Gabrielle said.

But the piglet didn't respond. He just took a sip from a glass of swill, picked up the phone and started dialling.

Gabrielle and I stormed out of his office and as we passed Mr Tosser's secretary, we looked into sympathetic eyes. Then, she handed us a note. It read: '*I'll* call the plumber for you. Let me handle it.'

And when we pulled up in front of Villa Alberto, two friendly guys from Gary's Plumbing were already digging a trench in the driveway between our house and Snake's house and undoing outflow pipes and doing up intake pipes, and doing whatever the heck it is that plumbers do to make everything in your life wonderful. And within an hour I was scrubbing the tub again. And we were happy. Some folk are good. Why couldn't the man have just picked up the phone? A rich man who needs to trample the little people has seriously twisted issues.

After I finished the tub we turned on the Weather Channel. The Tropical Wave has grown into a Tropical Depression. What this means is a series of thunderstorms has come together -- under ideal atmospheric conditions -- and stayed together for a long enough time and there is now organised circulation (as in 'rotation'). The Weather Channel goes on to say this mass of violence is feeding off the warm tropical waters, sucking up energy and moving slowly to the west. Winds associated with this meteorological demon are currently 23 to 39 miles per hour.

We watched some more and learnt that -- regarding impacting Florida -- wind shear can chop these monsters apart, the rotation of the earth makes them want to jog to the north and something called a Bermuda High, a high pressure over, well, Bermuda will fend them off to the south.

Gabrielle and I looked at each other. It could be blown apart, forced to the north towards the UK or pushed to the south.

'Crikey,' Gabrielle said, 'they don't have a clue where it's going.'

The next day we rode our bikes over to Alberto's gallery on Duval and sat in the cool shade of the Banyan Tree and drank *café con leche* with Alberto.

'Did you ever have any trouble with your toilet?' I asked.

'Always. Backed up in tub,' Alberto confessed.

Gabrielle asked Alberto how he dealt with his old landlord when annoying problems arose.

'Go to secretary,' he said. 'She no like him no more than we do. Think he *apiccicoso*.'

'A pitch-she what?'

'*Apiccicoso*.'

'What's *apiccicoso* mean?'

'Don't know in English, but big pain in backside.'

'That's him, all right,' Gabrielle said. 'A big pain in backside.'

Alberto introduced us to the fellow who worked at the open-air booth next door to Alberto's galley. The guy's name was Angelito and he was from Cuba. Angelito rolled cigars right there in front of the tourists and it was fascinating to watch someone skilled in this delicate art.

(FYI: At the turn of the century -- 1900 (*that* century) -- Key West was the nation's number one producer of Havana cigars and today as a result of that industry the island is awash with Cuban descendants. Cuba's Ten Years' War -- which began against Spain in 1868 -- forced thousands of Cuban cigar workers to flee across the Florida Straits to America. Situated within striking distance of Havana, Key West was a natural port o' call where artisans could escape Spanish oppression and continue to roll the prized Vuelta Abajo tobacco that made Cuban cigars the best in the world. In just over 20 years, Key West had transformed itself from a sleepy fishing village to a primary producer of Havana cigars.

With Cuban workers rolling Havana tobacco in less-taxed Key West, manufacturers were able to produce the best cigars at two-thirds the cost of production in Cuba. As opportunities rose, people poured in. Key West's population grew from 700 in 1840 to more than 18,000 in 1890, with Cubans by far the cultural majority.

Today, the Cuban influence remains strong with Cuban-owned restaurants, coffee shops, bakeries and cigar rollers such as Alberto's neighbour, Angelito.)

Angelito smiled a lot. And he laughed a lot. It was his way of communicating, you see, he only spoke five words of English: 'Hello, my very good friend.'

Angelito was one of those blokes who truly loved life. Every minute of it. And everything about it. And you would too if you had been in his sandals, you see, three years earlier Angelito and four of his friends set off from a beach near Havana on a raft made of inner tubes with planks lashed to the top. They were at sea for eight days, out of water, dehydrated and scorched delirious by the blinding sun. On the ninth day, one of Angelito's friends slipped overboard 'to drink' and was never seen again. On the tenth day, a shark took another right off the top of the raft. On the eleventh day, Angelito and the two remaining friends had America in sight, but they were intercepted by an American Coast Guard boat and taken to the American Naval Base on Cuba, at Guantanamo Bay, and imprisoned 'for their own protection against travelling the high seas in unseaworthy craft'. Angelito and his two mates spent two years living in a musty tent, until they were repatriated across the barbed wire and back to Cuba. Back in his homeland, and once again under Castro's long shadow, Angelito wasted no time and within a year, he and his two surviving friends set off on inner tubes once again. On day one, they saw a Cuban gunboat, but they were low to the water and went unnoticed. On day two, the sharks came and tried to take them off their raft, but they were ready this time and fought the sharks off with machetes. On day three, they almost lost their lives in the middle of the night in tempestuous seas. And then, on day four, their luck changed. The storm had pushed them close to the archipelago that is the Florida Keys, and on day five they stepped, dry-footed, on to American soil.

And now Angelito rolls cigars on Duval Street in Key West and lives in a one-room apartment with the two other Cubans who made the passage.

And Angelito rides his bike to work.

And smiles and laughs a lot.

And says: 'Hello my very good friend' a lot.

And means it.

* * *

When Gabrielle and I returned home from Alberto's, we readied ourselves to go down to Mallory even though we knew business was going to be nonexistent. We had the telly on in the background listening to the weather when the Tropical Update came on. The Tropical Depression's winds had increased 'sustained 45-miles-per-hour' and it had strengthened into a Tropical Storm. And the National Hurricane Centre in Miami had given it a name. The Tropical Storm was now known as 'Georges'.

* * *

WHAT NOBODY WILL TELL YOU: Since 1953, Atlantic tropical storms have been named from lists originated by the National Hurricane Centre and are now maintained and updated by an international committee of the World Meteorological Organization. The lists featured only women's names until 1979, when men's and women's names were alternated. Six lists are used in rotation. Thus, for example, the 2008 list will be used again in 2014.

The only time there is a change in the list is if a storm is so deadly, or costly, that the future use of its name on a different storm would be inappropriate for reasons of sensitivity. If that occurs, then at an annual meeting by the World Meteorological Organization committee the offending name is stricken from the list and another name is selected to replace it.

Gabrielle and I both hoped that 'Georges' would not end up being stricken from the list.

CHAPTER 14

Gabrielle still does not possess a work permit.

And now there's been a sweep by Immigration at the Ocean Key Resort and they've hauled off half of the Housekeeping staff and all of the employees who toiled in the hotel's Laundromat. The illegal workers were not allowed to return to their living quarters to pack a bag. And they were not allowed to telephone loved ones. They were frogmarched on to a bus and transported to a Miami detention centre where they awaited deportation.

We would travel to Miami to apply for a work permit, but we are afraid the authorities will arrest us and throw us in jail. A jail cell in Miami doesn't sound so very appealing.

We see Border Patrol and Immigration Agents skulking about on Duval all the time now. And their modus operandi is anything but high-tech. An officer simply approaches, asks where you are from, and if you have any accent other than American, you'd better have an ID handy and either flight tickets back home, or a visa.

Gabrielle's working hard to perfect an American accent, but it's been a tough slog, so we've decided to mirror the ANGELITO SCHOOL of LANGUAGES. This means she's only going to learn how to speak with an American accent using five words -- of street patois. We are still trying to decide what those five words will be. The short list includes: 'Chicago. How 'bout dem Cubbies?' or 'Brooklyn, on Toity-Toid Street?' or 'N'Orleans, sugar, tried da' gumbo?'

The other day, two gung-ho Border Patrol officers walked right past us and up to the Jet-Ski booth by the glass-bottom boat at the foot of Duval. Standing there, on the telephone, listening intently, not speaking, was one of the owners, Sean. Sean had just returned from a Jet-Ski tour around the island, so he was bare-chested, bare-footed and extremely tanned. In fact he looked almost, say, Cuban. But Sean is not from Cuba. He's from Wyoming.

One of the intrepid Border Patrol approached Sean and asked where he was from and because Sean was on the phone, he just held up a hand and said nothing. The officer, who believed in zero-tolerance (read: zero patience), repeated the question, but louder. Much louder. It's the American way. Sean is not one to be hurried by anyone, so he just held up a hand with subtext that read: 'Will you leave me the fuck alone, can't you see I'm on the goddamn telephone!' Positive they had captured yet another illegal alien, and sure he was not speaking because he could not speak English, the Border Patrol officer asked again, but this time in Spanish: '¿De dónde es usted?'

Having had about enough of this nonsense, Sean turned to the two officers and said: 'Yo soy de Wyoming.'

You see, Sean had been in the United States Coast Guard and had been working the waters between Florida and Cuba, of all places. And Sean, from Wyoming, was fluent in Spanish.

And that was the end of that.

* * *

If you go into one of your favourite pubs, late, and you can't find a seat, not to worry, just yell IMMIGRATION! at the top of your lungs and half the place will empty.

* * *

After we got back home from Mallory Square tonight, we grabbed Mr Leroy, settled on the couch and surfed for a good movie on the tube. You have so many choices in America. And there's so much crap.

Eventually we settled on that cult favourite *The Texas Chain Saw Massacre*. The movie is about a family of cannibals in Texas who 'more than make up in power tools what they lack in social skills'. This wasn't our first choice. Or our third.

The movie started, they rolled some credits, a little title music and then came the adverts. When the ads were over, the movie began again. Then there were more ads. Then more movie. Then more ads. We've been viewing ads sandwiched between bits and pieces of movie.

What is it about America and all those adverts?

Now, yet another advert has come on and it's more frightening than the movie. The ad is for lost souls suffering from depression. Eh? Does this fit the demographics for those of us watching this movie? Perhaps it does.

The ad extols the virtues of said depression drug, then in a rather sinister, sotto voce manner says: 'Side effects such as extreme agitation, the inability to sit still, jolting electric "zaps", dizziness, motor instability, extreme nausea, vomiting, high fever, abdominal discomfort, flu symptoms, anxiety, insomnia, aggression, nightmares, tremor, seizures, confusion, dependency, severe withdrawal and a "suicidal event" such as suicidal thoughts, suicidal gestures as in cutting of the body, suicide attempts and actual death...may occur.'

Crikey, if I had even a few of these side effects I'd be seriously depressed.

Gabrielle and I watched the rest of *The Texas Chain Saw Massacre* then, just before bed, we turned on the Weather Channel.

Tropical Storm Georges had strengthened into a 'Category 1' hurricane and was moving westward at 21 miles per hour, out over warm open ocean, 1300 miles east of the Lessor Antilles.

It was September 17th.

(FYI: All Hurricanes are dangerous, but some are more so than others. Storm-surge, wind, high tide, and various other factors determine the hurricane's destructive power. To make comparisons easier and to make the predicted hazards of approaching hurricanes clearer to emergency managers, National Oceanic and Atmospheric Administration's hurricane forecasters use a disaster-potential scale -- the eponymous 'Saffir-Simpson Scale'. This scale assigns storms to five categories and is used to give an estimate of the potential property damage and flooding expected along the coast from a hurricane.

The scale was formulated in 1969 by Herbert Saffir, a consulting engineer, and Dr. Bob Simpson, director of the National Hurricane Center in Miami. The World Meteorological Organization was preparing a report on structural damage to dwellings due to windstorms, and Dr. Simpson added information about storm surge heights that accompany hurricanes in each category.

Here are the five categories of the Saffir-Simpson Scale.

CATEGORY 1 -- Winds 74 to 95 miles per hour -- Damage: 'Minimal' -- Effects: 'No real damage to building structures. Damage primarily to unanchored mobile homes, shrubbery and trees. Also, some coastal road flooding and minor pier damage.'

CATEGORY 2 -- Winds 96 to 110 miles per hour -- Damage: 'Moderate' -- Effects: 'Some roofing material, door and window damage to buildings. Considerable damage to vegetation, mobile homes and piers. Coastal and low-lying escape routes flood 2-4 hours before arrival of center. Small craft in unprotected anchorages break moorings.'

CATEGORY 3 -- Winds 111 to 130 miles per hour -- Damage: 'Extensive' -- Effects: 'Some structural damage to small residences and utility buildings with a minor amount of curtainwall failures. Mobile homes are destroyed. Flooding near the coast destroys smaller structures with larger structures damaged by floating debris. Terrain continuously lower than five feet above sea level may be flooded inland eight miles or more.'

CATEGORY 4 -- Winds 131 to 155 miles per hour -- Damage: 'Extreme' -- Effects: 'More extensive curtainwall failures with some complete roof structure failure on small residences. Major erosion of beach. Major damage to lower floors of structures near the shore. Terrain continuously lower than ten feet above sea level may be flooded requiring massive evacuation of residential areas inland as far as six miles.'

CATEGORY 5 -- Winds greater than 155 miles per hour -- Damage: 'Catastrophic' -- Effects: 'Complete roof failure on many residences and industrial buildings. Some complete building failures with small utility buildings blown over or away. Major damage to lower floors of all structures located less than 15 feet above sea level and within 500 yards of the shoreline. Massive evacuation of residential areas on low ground within five to ten miles of the shoreline may be required.)

September 18th -- Gabrielle, Mr Leroy and I awoke to sunny skies, winds calm and the temperature already 80 degrees Fahrenheit.

We flipped on the Weather Channel and waited till 50-minutes past the hour and the Tropical Update. Georges had strengthened. It now had sustained winds of 105 miles per hour and it was a Category 2 hurricane. I looked over at my wife and she just stared back at me. We really didn't understand the ramifications.

September 19th -- Once again we awoke to glorious weather. And once again, the first thing we did was switch on the telly and wait for the Tropical Update. But we weren't ready for what we saw this morning: A reconnaissance aircraft had been sent into Hurricane Georges to measure wind speeds and atmospheric pressure. The winds were clocked at 150 miles per hour, atmospheric pressure at 938 millibars. Georges was now a powerful, perilous Category 4 hurricane. The Weather Channel tells us that a hurricane, with 150 mile per hour winds, packs the power equal to 200 times all the electricity being generated in the entire world.

(FYI: These reconnaissance aircraft are U.S. military aircraft and, as you can imagine, they are commanded by pilots with nerves of steel. 'Hurricane trackers' have been flying into the centres of hurricanes since the mid-1940s. Once inside -- if they make it -- they measure wind velocity and direction, the location and size of the eye, atmospheric pressure within the storm and its thermal structure. In the mid-1950s, a coordinated system of tracking hurricanes was developed, and it has greatly reduced the element of surprise, certainly something no one wants from a hurricane.)

September 20 -- Gabrielle and I wake up and we don't even wait to get out of bed. We'd moved the television into the bedroom the night before so we could zap it on first thing.

During the night, hurricane Georges has run into unfavourable conditions and the weatherman appears to have better colour in his cheeks than yesterday. A significant wind shear is breaking up the symmetry of the hurricane. Georges has weakened to a Category 2 hurricane and is now 585 miles southeast of San Juan, Puerto Rico. And were we ever glad. Not that we'd thought this monster was coming our way. It's just that we had never lived in this part of the world before and we weren't used to things that go tropical in the night.

That evening, to celebrate, we go to the Bull & Whistle and drink all their beer and most of their margaritas. There's no talk in the bar about Georges -- or what could have been.

September 21 -- We have a lie in, on account of all the beer and most of the margaritas. Eventually, Gabrielle turns on the Weather Channel, and our eyes bug right out of our aching heads. Hurricane Georges greets the day some 75 miles east of St. Croix, U.S. Virgin Islands. It has found warmer waters and the wind shear has disappeared. The winds can now circulate unimpeded around the eye of the storm. Georges has strengthened and it has been upgraded to Category 3. By 6 p.m, the eye is just off the east coast of Puerto Rico. Georges' winds are clocked at 115 miles per hour. Its gusts rise up to 150 miles per hour. Atmospheric pressure is 967 millibars. The diameter of the eye is between 20 and 25 miles wide. The hurricane passes over the island just to the south of the Cordillera Central, the island's central mountains. Intense thunderstorms, crushing rains and occasional tornadoes accompany the eye as it rakes across the island, moving at 15 miles per hour. At 8 p.m., the eye is 20 miles southwest of San Juan, where almost half of Puerto Rico's population live.

September 22 -- At 1 a.m. the eye leaves Puerto Rico to the west-southwest of Mayagüez, Puerto Rico's largest, west coast city. Hurricane Georges is the most devastating hurricane to hit Puerto Rico since 1932.

September 22 -- Before midday, Georges makes landfall in the Dominican Republic with winds of 120 miles per hour. Georges collides headfirst into the 10,414 foot Pico Duarte and the surrounding mountains, is ripped apart and begins to weaken. Nevertheless electricity is out in the entire country and won't be restored to full capacity for at least a month. The airport is heavily damaged and only open to military aircraft. Soldiers in Santo Domingo attempt to impose a curfew, but to little avail. Looters wade waist-deep in water, balancing televisions and air conditioners on their heads even as 110 mile per hour winds topple trees and crush houses. Bands of marauding youths with machetes and pistols roam the streets, many of them drunk. The death toll stands at 266.

In impoverished Haiti, the Peligre Dam, which is located on the border with the Dominican Republic, has not been able to accommodate flood waters and is overflowing. Reports are slow coming in from outlying villages that have suffered considerable devastation. Loss of life, 267.

We are getting worried again, so we call Popcorn Joe. Joe tells us not to worry and 'they never come this way'.

September 22 -- It's early evening in Cuba's five easternmost provinces and local Communist authorities trim tree branches, clean street drainage systems and order 30,000 school children down from mountain zones where they are helping to pick coffee.

September 23 -- A markedly diminished Georges makes landfall in eastern Cuba in the afternoon with winds near 75 miles per hour.

September 24 -- A minimal hurricane or not, Georges pounds Cuba with torrential rains, affecting the already drought ravaged provinces of Guantanamo, Holguin, Granma, Santiago de Cuba, Las Tunas and Camaguey. Reports show that 711,000 persons are evacuated to shelters, and 10,000 homes, two hospitals and 49 schools are damaged. Various economic facilities and 50 agricultural centres are destroyed. There is significant damage to sugar, coffee and banana crops, which will reduce foreign exchange earnings. Four people die in the storm when they are electrocuted by fallen power lines.

Gabrielle and I can't process what is unveiling before us. This evil, fickle mutation that had at one time seemed so distant and surreal was now posturing, blustering, at our back door. I cast my mind back to what I had read: 'Key West will never take a direct hit from a hurricane. The tall mountains of Cuba will tear it apart.'

But the mountains in Cuba weren't nearly as eminent and prodigious as those in the Dominican Republic.

And we were scared.

CHAPTER 15

September 24 -- Georges continues to hug the Cuban coastline. Forecasters in Miami fear that not only will it redevelop, but it could threaten the Florida Keys. Emergency management personnel begin immediate evacuations from Key West and the Lower Keys so no one will get caught in a logjam on the narrow Overseas Highway.

The director of the National Hurricane Centre in Miami goes on television: 'This storm looks like it's all set to explosively intensify once the eye gets back over open water.'

He then urges stragglers in Key West and the rest of the Keys to get out: 'We're extremely concerned that the land areas will be inundated with water and we'll lose a lot of folks down there.'

In Key West, hospital patients and the elderly are being airlifted out of harm's way.

Gabrielle and I don't know what to do. We only have bicycles. How are we going to escape the epic wrath of Georges?

We telephone Popcorn Joe. He's staying put, but he tells us to get out.

We telephone Alberto. He and his family are afraid they'll get stranded on the Overseas Highway and drown.

We telephone around to the Car Rental Agencies and they are sold out (it was the first time the convertibles had been the last to go).

We call the airport only to learn the last flight out is overbooked.

We telephone Popcorn Joe again but he's not home. We bravely tell his answering machine that we are not able to evacuate Key West and we don't know what to do.

And now we are frightened out of our skins.

We turn on the Weather Channel and some of the best meteorologists in the business can't say for certain where Georges is going to make landfall. The unknown factor makes it all the more stressful.

We hear a loud knock at our backdoor and we jump, but it's just Popcorn Joe. He has a big smile on his face and that makes us feel a lot better.

'Got something for ya,' he says.

We go around to the side of our house where Joe has parked his pickup. Our friend has hauled over ten large sheets of plywood for us so we can board up our windows.

'Board 'em up good and tight,' Joe says. And then he looks up at our palm tree: 'And you'd better cut those new coconuts down.'

It takes us a couple of hours to board up our windows with the aid of an electric screwdriver. Mrs Grace across the lane and Snake, next door, have chosen to ride it out, so we help them board up, as well. Then we ride our bikes over to the bank to withdraw some cash and head over to Fausto's market to buy drinking water and other supplies. When we get to the market, we are shocked by what we see. Many of the shelves have been stripped bare. We purchase some candles and a couple gallons of water, matches and some mysterious cans of food you would never buy unless there was a hurricane on the way.

Then we go home, fill up our bathtub with water and take down our beloved hammock.

Late that afternoon, we ride our bicycles down Duval. Key West is devoid of life forms (I know what you're thinking-- you're thinking it's usually that way anyhow. Ha ha). Most of the establishments are boarded up. Sandbags have been placed in front of doorways.

We pedal our bikes out to Higgs Beach. We are the only ones there. Even the seagulls know something is up and have flown off in search of safe harbour. The wind is eerily calm. The air is sticky and heavily laden, a reminder that weather from the tropics is coming. We look out in the direction of Cuba. The heavens are moody and presage ill fortune. An insatiable beast is just out there, growing, strengthening as it spreads our way. The first outer bands could be reaching us later tonight.

We go home and sit out on our back deck with Mr Leroy. I pick up a book about Hemingway and Key West entitled *Papa*. The author, James McLendon, has a bit in there about a hurricane that had hit in 1935. It was the worst hurricane to ever hit the Florida Keys. 'It struck Upper and Lower Matecumbe Key and killed or obliterated most everything in its path. The hurricane had stalled in the Atlantic off the Keys and gathered a monstrous strength the Keys had not known in all their recorded history. On the morning of September 2nd, 1935, the barometer dropped and dropped and from out of a driving rainstorm at the outer edge of the hurricane, a 200-mile-an-hour killer wind emerged from a barometer reading of 26.35 (892 millibars) the lowest ever recorded in the hemisphere. A 17-foot tidal wave crashed over the Keys and when it was all over, there was nothing but devastation. A rescue train, dispatched from Miami to evacuate local families in Key West, lay in a swirling mass of steel, its passengers dead, blown into the Gulf of Mexico or tangled in the mangroves. In all, 577 bodies were finally accounted for, but the true number of the dead was never known.'

I put the book down. This is not what I need right now.

I go inside and get the cat's-eye seashell Shark-Man gave us and place it in my pocket. Then I make some Cuban coffee.

And then Gabrielle brings Mr Leroy inside and we sit on the bed in a house with all the windows boarded-up, and we turn on the Weather Channel and watch a hurricane as big as the state of Texas bearing down on an island not much bigger than Hyde Park. Will Key West take a direct hit? That's the question, but no one has an answer. Not yet. The Weather Channel that had once been a source of amusement has now become our friend. It is our link with brainy, vigilant folk who understand these restive demons and that nearly comforts us.

We switch on our little portable radio and tune in a local station. An unnerved voice tells an enraptured listening audience a curfew has been imposed for later that evening. Gabrielle and I give each other a look, we place Mr Leroy on the bed, leave the TV on for him (the Animal Channel) and bolt for the Bull.

And the Bull is open!

We take a seat at the bar. It's hot and sticky in here. I look around. Business is slow, and that comes as no surprise, but the few patrons present are making up for those who haven't shown by really knocking back the plonk.

There's no music and the atmosphere is decidedly morose. I've never been in an establishment where alcohol is being served that is so subdued. We're told that 'hurricane parties' are traditionally quite lively. Something has these folk spooked.

We order drinks and hold them close to the chest as if they were our best friends. We talk to total strangers at the bar and we let go with little nervous laughs. Then the place goes quiet when our brains spring back to reality. And then we order more alcohol. Then we talk a lot and share our concerns. Somehow it makes us feel better to commiserate with other sad, terrified souls like ourselves.

Just before curfew, we scarper.

We hurry down Duval, and the streets are empty and the wind has picked up. The feeling is not unlike running down a dangerous dark alley you've never been down before. We keep looking over our shoulders, but there's no one else out there -- or is there?

Mr Leroy is asleep when we get home, so we flip to the Weather Channel. Hurricane Georges has taken an unexpected turn towards the west and to our horror the eye is now taking dead aim at Key West.

We watch the massive festering form of Georges on the radar, stretching from south of Cuba to the Florida peninsula. And to our vexed brains, Georges seems alive now. A behemoth Pacman gobbling up everything in its path as it churns towards the Southernmost point of the contiguous United States.

And then we fall asleep.

Gabrielle and I are rudely awakened by high winds, lightning and abnormally heavy rain. We shuffle in the dark to our front room and peer out through a little crack the plywood has not covered and are shocked to see bright flashes of purple light split the sky. Power transformers are exploding. Lightning strikes with a deafening concussion and it's followed by a high voltage bang. In front of our little cottage a severed power line snakes along the lane spitting fire. And then we hear the most terrifying sound of all: the simple, innocuous CLICK as our air conditioner dies. The power is out, Key West has been severed from the mainland and our island world has been plunged into total blackness.

We shuffle back and grab Mr Leroy and light some candles and hover around our portable radio. A disembodied voice tells us the Keys are taking a beating. The first outer bands of Georges have just reached Marathon (50 miles up the Overseas Highway) and touched off a waterspout.

It's a couple of hours later now, and the batteries in the radio are dying (we failed to purchase spare batteries). We think it might be sunrise soon, but we're not sure. The wind continues to pick up and the rain lashes our tin roof as a ship's officer might flog an AWOL sailor.

Something outside has broken. I peek out the crack in the front but can't see anything other than rain blowing sideways.

We are not happy. We fear a tornado will spawn from this nightmare.

Our roof has sprung a leak right over our computer, so I put the oscilloscope in two garbage bags and tie it all up.

The wind builds and builds and builds and we wonder if our paper-thin walls will hold, then the wind subsides and just when we catch our breath, it begins to build all over again. It's as if we are riding a roller-coaster, but each time we go around we climb higher and fall farther.

There is a rat moving about behind the walls. Mr Leroy shows no interest and is not leaving Gabrielle. I can't blame him.

Our food is spoiling. The refrigerator was a poor excuse for refrigeration at best and now we've had no power for hours.

It's flooding outside. I know this because I can hear the rain now crashing into water that floods our lane. I peer out the crack and everything out there looks dark green, not unlike our kitchen used to look before I painted it.

A tremendous crash on the front of the house! We have no clue what that was.

For sure it's daylight now. It's still greenish-black out there, but I can see things sailing down the lane: dustbin lids, a gigantic palm frond, bits of tin roofs.

We hear glass breaking, but it's not coming from our house.

If possible, the wind has increased. Now it's howling. Screeching. A banshee. The Harpies. This is Hades on earth and we are all just a little freaked out. How long can this go on?

Another crash! Something resembling our fence is floating down the lane.

We're beyond nervous. Our synapses are sizzling circuits. We wish we had evacuated. Carrying Mr Leroy we run back and forth to peep out the crack. The tree across the lane is bent sideways and coconuts shoot by like cannonballs. I forgot to cut down the coconuts!

Now we can hear more than one rat running behind the walls.

Gabrielle and I are telling each other jokes and we are so shell-shocked we are laughing like hyenas. This is the scariest thing we've ever been through in our lives.

The wailing, moaning wind grows and grows and grows. Louder than ever before. Different than before. Deafening now. A baneful roar that is threatening to blow our house down. Then we hear a horrific splitting sound and there's a tremendous crash on our roof.

And our front door explodes open.

And the maelstrom extinguishes our candles.

We rush to the door and try to force it closed, but the storm fights back. Both of us have our shoulders into the door and we're pushing with all our might, but Georges is pushing back with unnatural strength, his evil fingers trying to gain entry. The blast is so relentless we have to lie flat on our backs and use our legs to wedge the door shut.

'Can you hold it on your own?' Gabrielle asks. 'I'm going to go fetch the hammer.'

And as I'm prone on the floor bench-pressing it with my legs, Gabrielle nails the door shut. Not an easy task in the dank black pit that is our domicile.

We both collapse on the floor, drenched, soaked to the skin.

We breathe a big sigh of relief and let go with a nervous laugh. And then we laugh long and hard, but then we stop. And do you know why? We stop because that's when Gabrielle says to me: 'Where's Mr Leroy?'

Frantic, I claw at the nails with the hammer. Each one rips out with a submissive moan. Why do nails go in easily, but are so damn hard to extract?

I jerk the last nail out and the door explodes in again. The outside world is a smeared tropical netherworld of mysterious flying objects, slanting black rain and apocalyptic sounds.

I call to Mr Leroy.

He's nowhere to be seen.

Gabrielle calls.

Nothing.

We're climbing the walls.

Outside our front door, a fetid, toxic cesspool surges against our threshold -- a putrid cocktail of sewage, coconuts and wheelie bin flotsam.

But there is no sign of Mr Leroy. Where did the poor little fellow go? He won't stand a chance in these conditions.

I stick my head out and peer down the steamy lane from hell.

Gabrielle screams: 'Look!'

Not out in the elements, rather standing behind us with a look of 'Will you please close the flipping door!' is Mr Leroy.

I fight the door shut again and Gabrielle is about to begin pounding bent nails, when we realise something quite uncanny is occurring -- the wind is dissipating, flagging, weakening. And then suddenly it stops.

Cautiously, I crack the door and then Gabrielle picks up Mr Leroy and we all peep out. It's a miracle! There is no rain and there is no more danger. We are joyous. We hug each other and almost flatten Mr Leroy.

We stand there Glory be! dumb-struck for the longest time and then something even stranger occurs: Just the smallest patch of blue appears well to the south and the sun peeks through.

'It's over!' I shout. 'We've survived hurricane Georges!'

We wade out our door and can't believe what we see. Our plumeria tree has snapped in half, our seven-foot wooden fence is nowhere to be seen and so is all the gravel we had sewn in our driveway.

One by one our neighbours emerge from their boarded-up homes up and down the lane and we all stand there in semi-sunshine, calm wind, complete stillness -- gobsmacked.

Mrs Grace across the lane looks to the heavens, mumbles something in Spanish and crosses herself. Snake to our left gives us a big smile and blows out his cheeks. The Pig-Man appears with a potbellied Vietnamese pig that seems to desperately need to squat in the deep grass. The Bitch-Bovine across the way pokes her head out and checks on her car.

After a short time we lose the sun and the patch of blue, then we lose the bright ethereal light and slowly an all too familiar oppressive green hue appears.

Gabrielle and I slosh our way over to Snake: 'What's going on?'

'That was the eye passing over. You'd better get back inside. We're gonna get hit by the back end of the storm now,' he says.

'But we thought it was all over,' I whine.

'The wind is going to come from completely the opposite direction. We're only halfway through this.'

'What time is it?' Gabrielle asks.

'Just after noon.'

The hurricane had been raging for eight hours -- and we have eight more hours to go. We're not so sure we're ready to climb back on the roller-coaster.

We go back inside, find some new candles and then drive the first nail in the front door.

We hear a knock and Snake's small voice: 'Forget about the front door. Nail the back one.'

'Thanks, Snake,' I yell. Good neighbours are hard to come by.

We nail the back door shut. Once again we are entombed in a black box. And we're dripping in sweat. There is not a breath of fresh air in the house.

But we're not as nervous now. We lived through the front half, so there's a good chance we will survive the back half: Georges Part II, the sequel.

If you want to know what the back half of Georges was like for us, go back and reread the previous pages, take out the bit about the front door exploding open -- and add the snake. That's right, there's a snake in the house with us now. He must have crawled in to escape the flooding. How he slithered in we don't know. The only thing we *do* know is that he's big -- alarmingly big. At least five feet long. And thick. And no it's not the large black rat snake. This snake is a sickly yellow. The colour of the patients in the jaundice ward. We saw him by candle light over in the corner and now he's gone.

What if he's venomous? I can't exactly fire up the oscilloscope and Google him right now to find out, can I? So we sit on barstools with our feet up off the floor in the dark suffocating heat and listen to the Harpies.

With the wind screeching and hissing at us from 180 degrees the opposite direction now, different parts of the house are being stressed and the roof is leaking like a sieve from just about everywhere except where I patched it.

Our bed is wet. And our futon is wet. We don't know what we'll do when it's time to go to bed, not that we'd sleep anyway what with a five-foot, forked-tongue, thick-as-your-leg, jaundice-coloured reptile in situ.

I need the loo but I'm afraid to venture off my chair. An hour passes, but I don't. The situation is becoming grave. The romance of riding out the second half of the hurricane departed with the arrival of the snake.

'Take the machete and the candle,' Gabrielle suggests. 'Tap the floor in front of you as you go.'

I'm now sitting on the commode and the rain is pounding the tin roof over my head. It doesn't sound like rain, it sounds like ball bearings. What's worse, every horror story I've ever heard about snakes coming up through toilets is popping into my brain. I don't tarry.

I flush the toilet. On account of the bathtub being filled with water and plugged, and the streets being flooded, the toilet backs up and overflows on to the bathroom floor.

I take my position back atop my barstool. The air is dead and enervating on the inside, but sounds like a jet engine on the outside. And we are miserable.

We wish we had never left Glasgow. Back there our only worry had been if we would get a table at Dhabba in Merchant City, or not.

Later I arm myself with the machete and tap my way to the kitchen. In the kitchen, I can hear an awful sound. I can hear it in spite of the wind. A rat trying to gnaw through the wall. He wants in, desperately. The rising flood waters must have him trapped on a support beam under our house and his only hope for survival is to break into our kitchen. With each gnaw wood splinters. I kick the shit out of the wall and the noise stops. I hear the frantic scurrying of little rodent feet with toenails that need to be clipped.

Still fumbling around in the black hole that is our kitchen, I'm unable to open any of the hurricane provisions because we only have an electric can opener, so we dine on nameless muck out of a tube. We aren't very hungry. Even Mr Leroy, who is usually an eating machine, is off his feed.

Over the course of the next few hours our roof takes a crushing blow, a missile of some sort pierces the sheet of plywood covering the kitchen window, shattering the glass, and an ungodly shrill screech emanates from behind the walls. We think the snake is back there and has offed one of the rats.

The wind is noticeably stronger than before. It's shaking the house the way a Jack Russell shakes, say, a cornered rat. Just when we're wondering how much more our besieged cottage can take, there is a climatic crescendo of Georges' fury, the carnage outside subsides and the wind dissipates.

The fever has broken.

We're startled by a pounding sound at the back door, then soothed by the accompanying voice: 'It's over! It's over now!'

We extract the nails from the back door, fling it open and see our neighbour standing there. 'You can come out now,' Snake says. 'Everything's gonna be hunky-dory.'

We are so happy we hug Snake. He knew we were afraid.

Gabrielle picks up Mr Leroy and we tiptoe out into our submerged backyard and peer into the darkness. It's after 9 p.m., and even though there is not a light anywhere, we are shocked by what we see. We see the sky. Our backyard used to be a tangled boscage of tropical splendour, but now it's a bare-naked skeleton. One of our palm tress has been blown down and has crushed the roof. A deciduous tree has been completely uprooted. Many of the other trees are standing, but nary a leaf remains.

The lane out front is still awash with filthy water. Power lines are down. Gnarled branches form a gigantic game of pick-up-sticks. We hear someone in the distance crying. We see the beam of a lonely torch off towards Whitehead Street. The air is heavy and smells of the sea -- and petrol.

It's been a hellish ordeal.

It's been 17 hours.

The only good that has come from sinister Georges' siege of the island is this: A massive oak was uprooted and crushed the Bitch-Bovine's BMW.

In our flippies, we start to venture down towards Whitehead Street, but there's lethal debris everywhere. It's as black as the inside of your auntie Emma's larder and impossible to see where we're going. We spot more snakes, so we turn back.

In the distance we hear a policeman on a bullhorn advising of the curfew.

We are exhausted from lack of sleep and sheer fright. But we don't know where we're going to sleep. The house is a gagging sauna, our bed and futon are soaked and we still don't know where you-know-who is.

Gabrielle gets an idea: 'Let's put our hammock back up and sleep up off the ground. It will be cooler outside. And safer.'

My wife! Not only good-looking, but creatively intelligent, as well.

We tie one end of our hammock around the remaining palm tree and the other end we attach to our open back door. Then we crawl up into the hammock, get Mr Leroy settled and fall into a deep, clinically disturbed sleep.

We awake at sunrise to the sound of a chain saw coming from somewhere in the direction of the Pig-Man's house. Despite terrifying dreams, we slept well in the protective custody of our hammock, you see, the terrifying dreams were not as terrifying as the reality of the previous day.

We're thankful just to be alive.

We walk around the side of our cottage and we're stunned by the devastation that is now visible in the daylight. The back half of Georges did more damage than the front half. We knew most of the leaves on the trees were gone, but what we couldn't see the previous night was that the remaining leaves are brown and dead. It looks as if someone has poured acid on all the trees. We will learn later it was caused by the heavy salt content in the hurricane force winds.

The palm tree that fell upon our roof has crushed one corner. Our yard is a wasteland. There is detritus of every imaginable sort (and disgusting variety) everywhere. We slosh our way up to Whitehead Street and see someone riding a bicycle slowly past. The stranger waves and we wave back. We walk through a debris field the few blocks down to the Hemingway House. Winds have toppled a huge banyan tree that has stood nearly a century and a half.

Key West is a disaster.

When we get back home, we find that the interior of our house is a furnace. Without the shade trees the sun beats down mercilessly and has turned our home into the boiler room on a tramp freighter adrift in the doldrums.

'I better get the boards off and air out the house,' I say.

I fetch the electric screwdriver.

'You're going to need a heck of a long extension cord,' Gabrielle says. 'There's no power this side of the Miami airport.'

We'd had no experience with hurricanes and now we were paying for it.

I crack open the front door and we get the semblance of a sucking draft going between the front and back doors. We strip the bed and hang all the bedclothes out on a bare tree. Then we haul the mattress out, and finally the futon. The mattress is sodden and we can barely lift it. Take Two with the futon. And they both are mouldy. Ah, the tropics. We carry them around the side of the cottage and dump them in a growing pile of debris to be picked up by the city.

We really don't have the money to buy new furniture.

Key West fires up its emergency generator and we now have brownouts and rolling blackouts (and that's the good news), and we're able to get the boards off the windows. But the damage has been done. The dank, airless confines of our cottage have been turned into a gigantic Petri dish and every conceivable mould and bacterial culture has taken root in our home. To add to the rich aroma, a rat has indeed died behind the walls (presumably a homicide).

Our cottage is unlivable and we continue to sleep outdoors in the sanctuary of our hammock. To conserve power, no one is allowed to use air conditioners, and the nights are still and serene and hearken back to a time of a backwater island void of juddering A/C units cranking out upwards of 24000 BTUs.

And, no, we still haven't seen that snake.

Speaking of snakes, we decide to pay a visit to our landlord. He, no surprise, has not been by to check on us or his property.

We tell Mr Tosser about all the damage: the trees, the fence, the mould, the mildew, the buggered window in the kitchen. And do you know what he says to us?

'Buy what you need. Fix what you want. Bring me the receipts. Insurance will cover everything.'

Gabrielle and I do a double take. Did a coconut fall on his head during the hurricane?

Key West was void of tourists, so there was no work at the Pineapple Guest House and there were no sales down at Mallory. We used the days to refit Villa Alberto. We built a new fence, washed the entire interior with trisodium phosphate to kill the mould, touched up the outside with paint, fixed the leaky roof and replaced the pane of glass in the kitchen window.

The stench of the rotting rat eventually dissipated, the swirling ceiling fans kept any fresh mould at bay and Popcorn Joe provided us with a spare mattress so we were able to sleep once again inside our home.

We spent a fair amount of money we didn't have to get Villa Alberto back up and running and our modest funds were drying up. Thank goodness Mr Tosser had come to his senses and we would soon be reimbursed.

Gabrielle paid a visit to our bank to move a few hundred dollars out of our not-to-be-touched savings account and was startled to find our savings no longer existed.

Four-thousand dollars was missing. Someone had emptied our account. And we had only $30 to our name.

CHAPTER 16

Gabrielle came home nearly in tears, grabbed me and we both rushed right back to the bank.

At the bank, a customer-service agent, who seemed rather insensitive to our plight, presented us with a photo copy of a document.

'What's this?' I asked.

'It's a wire transfer requesting four-thousand dollars.'

Gabrielle and I studied the wire transfer.

'This was sent from New York,' Gabrielle said.

'And?' minimum-wage brain said.

'We weren't in New York.'

'All I can tell you is, when a wire transfer comes through with the correct account number and the account holder's signature, we act on it.'

'But we don't live in New York. We live in Key West. Three blocks from here, actually. Didn't that set off an alarm bell? Why didn't someone pick up the phone and check?'

No response.

Instead of being on our side and helping us solve this terrifying development, the customer-service agent seemed determine to make the situation even worse: 'Is this your signature, Mrs Breakfield?'

We studied the signature. It was Gabrielle's signature. No doubt about it.

'Looks like it, yes, but I didn't authorise this transfer.'

'Well, as far as we are concerned, you did.'

We didn't like this response, and we didn't like this woman, so we asked to see the bank manager.

'He's not back yet,' minimum-wage-brain told us. 'He evacuated.'

'I bet he did,' Gabrielle said. 'When will he be back?'

'Not sure. Seventh of October, I think.'

Gabrielle and I studied this woman as we had studied the wire transfer -- long and hard. Where was the support? Where was the loyalty? What was the motto at this bank, 'The customer always comes last'?

The woman must have felt the points of our curare-dipped daggers, for she bleated 'If you'll just excuse me' and picked up the copy of the wire transfer and disappeared into the area of the vault.

Stay tuned.

* * *

Key West didn't open back up for business until the 5th of October, ten long days after Georges' visit. Then the roadblock into the Keys was dropped, the 11 p.m. to 6 a.m. curfew lifted and alcohol flowed deep into the night. Tourism, the lifeblood of this part of the world, began to trickle back in and with the infusion of tourists business at Mallory and the guest house started to pick back up.

But we were still struggling to get by.

On the morning of seven October, now desperate, we paid another visit to the bank.

The original customer-service agent wasn't there ('She's on vacation'), so we had to explain our story all over again. Then we asked to see the manager.

'The bank manager is upstairs in a meeting.'

'We'll wait,' Gabrielle said.

'It may take a while.'

'We'll wait,' Gabrielle said.

And wait we did. After two hours, I approached a different minimum-wage employee and asked after the bank manager and was told: 'Oh, he just went to lunch. Should be back in an hour or so.'

More than three hours after we first arrived at the bank, the minimum-wage clone we had dealt with three hours earlier materialised holding a copy of the wire transfer.

'Where's the manager?' Gabrielle asked.

'Busy. But he said you could have a look at the wire transfer.'

'We've already seen it,' Gabrielle said. 'We want to speak with the manager.'

And do you know how this customer-service slug responded? 'Oh, nobody really gets to see the manager.'

'Oh, you mean nobody with just zippo in their account,' Gabrielle said.

The arrogant look the woman had on her face suddenly deteriorated to one that people get when they step in dog shit.

About now, Gabrielle spotted something we hadn't seen the last time. With her eyes she directed me to the wire transfer. And then I saw it. Scribbled in a lonely corner was the name of the person who had authorised the transfer. And the name was none other than that of the invisible bank manager.

'May we take this home?' Gabrielle asked.

'Not allowed out of the bank,' the slug said.

And I don't know what suddenly came over me, but I snatched the coveted document out of the customer-service agent's hand, shot her a look of 'don't even think about it' and then escorted my wife to the front door.

Outside, Gabrielle stopped for a moment, gave me a bemused look and said: 'Wow!'

We pedalled our bikes back home, pulled out a copy of our bank statement, made two Cuban coffees and climbed up in our hammock. We always did our best thinking in the hammock.

Mr Leroy jumped up to consult and over the next hour we stared doggedly at the copy of the wire transfer. We concluded that Gabrielle's signature was in fact so authentic it had to be hers. Someone had scanned her signature. Then we had a good hard look at the account number and noticed that in fact it had two rogue 'zeroes' after a suspect 'hyphen'. And then we noticed something we hadn't spotted earlier, the date the wire transfer took place -- it was the day before hurricane Georges had unleashed his ruinous ire on the island. And it was a day we had made a withdrawal from our chequing account so we would have cash to procure hurricane supplies. Gabrielle's signature would be on the withdrawal slip.

We left Mr Leroy dozing in the hammock and jumped back on our bicycles and scurried over to the Bank From Hell. As we blew in the front door, I saw the customer-service clone physically recoil in a distinctly reptilian manner.

We asked to see the manager again.

'He's in a meeting,' she said, eyeing us coldly.

This I found hard to believe, unless it was a conference call, as I could see him through the glass partition of his office sitting on his corpulent behind.

Gabrielle and I have unspoken communication. She needed only to give me a look and we were both bolting for the manager's office. Needless to say he was not pleased to see us barge through his ivory-tower door, and he seemed even less enamoured with our presence when we brought to his attention his name on the wire transfer and the fact Gabrielle could not have been at the American Express bank in Manhattan at the same time she was signing a withdrawal slip in the Bank From Hell, Key West, Florida, not quite the USA.

Despite being confronted with this irrefutable evidence, the Manager stalled: 'I'll have to have our security officers look into this. Leave me the copy and I'll see what I can do.'

'Why do you need the copy if you have the original?' Gabrielle asked.

No response.

I'm uniquely articulate in these circumstances, so I let Gabrielle do all the talking.

Gabrielle: 'When can we expect to hear from you?'

Manager: 'It could take some time.'

Gabrielle: 'Can you give me an idea.'

Manager: 'No, I can't.'

Gabrielle: 'And what are we supposed to do in the meantime?'

Manager: 'That's up to you...'

Gabrielle: 'Let me explain something to you. You may not have noticed, but we just had a Category 2 hurricane blow through here. Tourism is in short supply. We're making no money. And we've had to put out cash we don't have, to repair a house that is not ours, so we can sleep somewhere at night. This extracurricular agro we're getting from you is not something we need right now.'

Clearly, the manager was not used to being on the arse-end of a tongue-lashing.

Manager: 'I'll see what I can do.'

Gabrielle: '"I'll see what I can do" is not good enough.'

We pedalled home, fired up the computer and drafted a letter outlining in excruciating detail the flagrant cockups of the Bank From Hell, featuring in a starring role the ineptitude of the bank manager. Then we jumped on the Internet and found the name of the most notorious, blood-thirty, ambulance-chasing attorney in the greater Miami area.

Don't get me wrong here, we couldn't afford some shit-hot Miami lawyer who doubled-billed you when he was on the loo, but that didn't stop us from including his blustery name at the bottom of our threatening missive, did it?

We made copies, hurried to the post office and sent registered letters to the Bank From Hell's home office, head of security and the president of the Key West branch.

The letters arrived at the respective offices the next day and within 24 hours our $4000, plus interest (such as it was), was safe and sound back in our not-to-be-touched savings account.

We later learnt someone had pilfered our cancelled cheques out of our mailbox and that a fraud ring based in Nigeria was behind the entire scam.

And on account of, well, our account, the Bank From Hell no longer sends cancelled cheques through the post or accepts faxes as authorisation for wire transfers.

CHAPTER 17

'Fantasy Fest is coming! Fantasy Fest is coming!'

Forgive me for shouting this out with unbridled enthusiasm, but what Gabrielle and I could use right now is a really good party.

Even more importantly, the ten days of Fantasy Fest will pump eighteen-million dollars into the local economy at a time when we are, thanks to Georges, fresh out of local economy.

Since this was to be our first excursion into 'Key West's premier visitor attraction' we wanted to find out if the big event was all it was cracked up to be. And one of the best places to gage the quickening pulse of the island was at our local, the Bull.

We grabbed seats by one of the big windows that opened on to the street. It was the third week of October and still surprisingly balmy. What a climate! Up on stage, a band that looked as if it hadn't slept in a week was playing the odd song between breaks. Outside, Duval was awash with the incoming tide of Fantasy Fest revellers.

Gabrielle ordered some tropical concoction and I ordered a Budweiser. We watched this new wave of tourists stroll by and right off it was clear, these folk were of a different breed.

It was in their walk. It was in their dress -- or lack of it. It was in their decidedly non-sober state. Key West was being besieged by professional party animals.

As the night wore on and the booze flowed and uptight folk lightened up a notch or two, we asked some of the patrons around us if they were in town for Fantasy Fest. They all were. Then we asked what made Fantasy Fest so special that it attracted tourists from all over the globe.

'It's an adult Halloween with adult costumes.'

'It's the bawdy, bacchanal party of all parties!'

'It's a combination of Mardi Gras in New Orleans and Carnival in Rio, only kinkier -- and with phlegmatic police.'

'It's all jockstraps and G-strings!'

'It's body paint in lieu of clothing.'

'It's the best of Sodom and Gomorrah.'

'It's depravity in its purest form.'

I looked over at Gabrielle: 'They have parties like this? Have we been living in a cave? Certainly Fantasy Fest draws some normal folk?'

Gabrielle motioned with her eyes towards some ancient grey-haired gentleman sitting all alone at the bar. 'There's your answer. He's here for Fantasy Fest and he appears to be of normal lineage and passable mental health.'

I peered through the dark at the man. Sandals. Shorts. Tank top. A few strings of Fantasy Fest beads around the neck. Nothing unusual here. About now, the man got up from his stool and gave his seat to some young busty thing in a tube top who looked as if she'd just stepped out of the Jerry Springer Show. A conversation ensued. The elderly man whispered something in the young lady's ear, then placed a string of beads around her neck. The lass turned, looked right into the man's smiling face and slapped him silly.

'Whatever the question was,' Gabrielle said, 'that would be a NO.'

The old sod looked around the bar for another place to sit and I gestured to the stool next to me. I felt sorry for the old geezer, but as he approached I was shocked to see he had a pierced nipple. As my new best friend slipped on to the barstool next to me, I noticed he did so in a cautious manner that suggested his nipple wasn't the only body part pierced.

'I'm in town for Fantasy Fest!' he announced, devoting a bit too much time looking at Gabrielle. 'Best time of the year to be here.'

As my mission is to bring you the truth through accurate reportage, I asked this maven of the midway what his take on the Big Party was.

'Let me put it to you this way,' he said, with a noticeable Boston accent, 'if your mother weaned you too young and you have sexual predator tendencies, then this is the place and the time of the year for you.'

I glanced over at Gabrielle, then back at the octogenarian. 'And what might your purpose be here, if I may be so bold to ask?'

Mr Scrotal-Pierce's watery eyes cruised the dance floor for succulent prey then turned to me and said: 'Trading beads for a peek at some twenty-something flesh.'

'Cheque, please!'

Gabrielle and I bolted from the bar and headed up Duval. The air was hot and muggy and the whole town seemed to be out. This is the way it is in Key West. Every night, everyone is out and about trolling up and down Duval. It really makes for a wonderful atmosphere.

When we reached Petronia, we spotted streams of locals turning off Duval and heading down into Bahama Village.

Now what's going on?

We, too, peeled off and saw booths and food stands lining both sides of the street. We had stumbled upon an exotic Caribbean street party with island food, island music, island colours and island arts and crafts. This was Goombay Festival, a grassroots (read: grass) tribute to Key West's island heritage. If you hadn't felt you were on a Caribbean island when you first arrived in Key West, you sure did now. This

Fantasy Fest fringe festival had to be one of the great, best-kept secrets -- or perhaps it was just the two of us who didn't know.

We strolled down Petronia Street, deeper into Bahama Village and the deeper we went, the deeper we seemed to venture into the Caribbean. The atmosphere was electrifying and exotic back here, with all sorts of pungent island smells, and there was just the hint of, say, danger in that I don't think we would have been in this part of town had there not been this festival.

And the danger made the Caribbean experience all the more authentic.

It was nearly midnight when we arrived back home, grabbed Mr Leroy and crawled up into the hammock. We could hear a steel drum playing from Goombay in the distance. A light breeze brought the fragrance of jasmine. The stars were shining brightly here at the end of the world.

And our life was back to normal.

Happy once again, we drifted off to sleep in the hammock.

* * *

We awoke in our hammock one morning during Fantasy Fest with a bit of a start. There was a strange man standing over us. I blinked at the intruder. He looked somehow familiar but at first I couldn't place him. Then he presented his card. He was an estate agent. The same estate agent who had stopped by and complimented us during our upgrade of Villa Alberto.

He handed us a letter.

'Your landlord is selling off all the cottages he owns in the lane. Since your cottage is the most impressive, we're going to use yours as the model. My name's Bob. We've got viewings today at one and three.'

Flabbergasted, we watched as Bob hiked out through our just rebuilt back gate, climbed into his Mercedes and spat up some of our new gravel as he laid rubber out of the lane.

'The bastards!' Gabrielle hissed. 'The paint's not even dry from all the repairs we did around here!'

We looked back at our little cottage which we had come to love. We were shell-shocked.

I went inside and put on the kettle and then we climbed back up into the hammock, sipped our tea and sulked.

'What are we going to do if it sells,' my wife asked.

'Go directly to Mr Tosser's office and swing him around by the testicles, I reckon. He hasn't reimbursed us for our expenses yet and now he's using us. He should have been put down long ago.'

We fumed for the rest of the afternoon and then in the evening we dragged ourselves over to Duval to catch the famous Fantasy Fest parade and to forget about our woes for a few hours.

And forget about our woes we did almost immediately. As soon as we turned on to Duval from Southard, and entered into a tangled mass of skimpily dressed tourists, we came face to face with a blond Adonis rippling in glistening muscles. But that's not what caught our eye, what caught our eye was that he was wearing an enormous hat shaped like a penis.

'Look! A dickhead! Just like our landlord.'

We weaved our way through the throngs and thongs and I can tell you right off if you want to forget about your troubles for a while this is the place to be.

We fought our way to an outdoor stand and purchased open containers of alcohol (so we wouldn't stand out) and dived into a delirious mass of oversexed carbon-based life forms and were soon surrounded by 101 Dalmatians -- only this lot looked different than the ones in the movie -- the ones in the movie had spots all over, but these just had teeny spotted bikini bottoms and spotted floppy ears. That's it. The Dalmatians moved en masse in the direction of a man dressed as a fire hydrant and we forged our way on through a crush of skin.

Soon Duval Street was saturated with costumed revellers in various stages of undress -- and in various stages of being fucked up. And what one gobsmacked American couple noted as they walked by, we felt, summed up the evening's attire, or lack of it: 'Sure are a lot of tits and dicks.'

As we ploughed along, enjoying the colourful atmosphere, the drinks and the warm night air, we espied a woman, topless, with the upper part of her torso painted like the head of a lion. Extremely authentic looking, might I add, although the eyes were just a TITch far apart. Then we spotted women in G-strings with body paint, men in G-strings with body paint, a stunning whip-me-fuck-me dominatrix, lots of gays in drag, a man dressed as a peacock, a dog dressed as peacock, a flock of Parrot Heads outfitted in parrot-head G-strings and various other folk sporting rather creative fetish attire.

This was *not* your typical street party.

I consulted my watch. The great parade wasn't meant to start for a while, yet it seemed that everyone who owned a kinky costume (or felt the urge to undress) was now on the loose.

What atmosphere!

What decadence!

What the hell is that!

Coming towards us was a gigantic, eight-foot high -- and if you don't mind, I'll just whisper this -- walking VAGINA! Anatomically correct from the looks of it, as well. At least that's what somebody behind us said. No. Really. Someone said that.

'Cover thyself!' I wanted to shout it out. 'There's a gigantic penis on the loose.'

Can you imagine if the two met and hit it off? Bears some thought, wouldn't you say?

What a love story!

What romance!

I'm sure there's a movie in there somewhere. Think about it. He's from America and works as a test pilot for a condom manufacturer. She's from the UK and works for, say, Victoria's Secret. They meet at a Knickers Convention in Hythe, at the Imperial. Fall arse over teacup for each other.

Then a war somewhere in the world keeps them apart. But they have promised to meet again, one day -- preferably near the end of the movie -- on top of the Empire State Building (or in Blackpool at the Houndshill Mall). It's Valentine's Day. He shows, but she doesn't as there's a Gynaecologists' Convention in town and hailing a cab is just not an option. Just as we in the audience have given up hope and have gone for our third popcorn and some Smarties, she arrives, they exchange bodily fluids and live happily, albeit in seclusion, ever after in Brooklyn on Toity-Toid Street (or perhaps Torquay).

We can entitle the movie WHEN HAIRY SULLIED SALLY. No?

I verbalise this to Gabrielle and she gives me a playful shove. And groans.

Eventually the real parade began and we watched it with local families from the PG-rated curb on Whitehead Street in front of the post office, and then when the parade was over and the 70-odd elaborate floats had passed us by, we darted across the street, cut through the car park behind the La Concha hotel, stepped over two Dalmatians tongue-wrestling under a blanket behind a mini-van and watched most of it all over again on bacchanal Duval Street.

And then we struggled back home through the mass of panting, overheated humanity and crawled up in our hammock -- and the reality of losing Villa Alberto set back in again.

CHAPTER 18

Estate-agent Bob and the anal prospective buyers of Villa Alberto were traipsing through our house on a daily basis now, so we requested they take off their anal prospective-buyer shoes when they entered our cottage. We had grown weary of hoovering and mopping up after arrogant sods with disposable income.

Have you ever been involved, willingly or unwillingly, in the changing of title of your home-sweet-cottage? Did you notice how courteous and polite some folk were when they entered your precious domain? And did you notice how rude, pretentious and disrespectful others were?

We had an American couple from 'up north somewhere' pay us a visit too early one morning and while estate-agent Bob was showing the wife the kitchen, her useless husband used the loo without asking. Apparently he wanted to keep his pee-sortie top secret because he didn't lift the seat.

What kind of barbarians were these people?

On another occasion, a couple talked down to us as they picked through every inch of our cottage and then concluded, out loud, they 'could never live in such a dump'.

Barbarians!

And then, on yet another immemorable occasion, estate-agent Bob brought bottom feeders over when we weren't home and the vile curs checked their e-mails on our computer and then failed to change back whatever the heck it is that needs to be changed back.

Beyond barbaric!

After that violative episode, we forbade estate-agent Bob to ever enter our domicile without 24-hour-advanced notice, under penalty of kicking his fleshy rump around the block.

* * *

The first cold front of the season has swept through dropping a gentle shower and leaving behind piercing-blue skies and lower humidity. Imagine living somewhere, where a cold front *improves* the weather!

The weather is in fact so ideal, we can still run around in shorts and swim in the ocean and, yes, even sit outside at night in our hammock and watch the stars twinkle happily back.

The start of November is a glorious time of the year to be in Key West. And we would really be enjoying it, but we still haven't been reimbursed for our renovations and repairs on Villa Alberto. Don't you just hate it when you have to chase after someone for money?

We've telephoned Mr Tosser twice now and he's always -- you won't believe it -- in a meeting. And he has failed to return our calls. So yet again we climb on our bicycles and pedal wearily and warily over to his posh offices. We stroll in through his hardwood double doors and right off we can see from his bug-eyed expression that we are not welcome. So we take seats.

'We've come by to pick up our money.'

'Still haven't heard from my bookkeeper.'

'And when will you hear from him?'

'Hard to say. He's a busy man.'

Gabrielle gives me a look.

And then Mr Tosser adds: 'And I'm a busy man, too, now if you'll excuse me...'

Gabrielle and I have had it up to here. We rise to leave and Mr Tosser hits us with this: 'Don't forget your rent's due this week.'

Once again we're livid as we pedal back home.

When we get home two things of note happen: First, estate-agent Bob calls to tell us there will be a 'showing' the next afternoon, and we inform Bob that the 'afternoon' is not good for us as we have to donate a kidney and could you please reschedule and stick your head up where the light doesn't shine; and secondly, we have elected not to pay our rent. Actually, we've decided to go on the attack, we are sending Mr Tosser our rent in an envelope with accompanying cover letter, but we are going to forget to enclose the cheque. Then when he has his secretary call us to tell us of our error, Gabrielle, who writes the cheques, will be in a meeting.

We've purchased an answer phone with a small portion of the money we've saved by not paying our rent and now when estate-agent Bob telephones to schedule an appointment, we monitor, but we don't pick up. We never seem to be home. We can hear him bleating, braying and pleading -- from our sanctuary out in the hammock -- but we don't answer. Oh, no. And when estate-agent Bob comes by to try to catch us in situ, we distinctly recognise his oversized Michelin tires grinding on our freshly laid gravel drive and we grab Mr Leroy and bolt in the back door, lock it and then peer out the front window at estate closet-case Bob mumbling invectives to himself.

And we are happy once again.

The little people are winning.

And I'm taking my wife out to dinner tonight with more of the rent money.

Life is good.

Damn good.

* * *

Today is the 30th of November and as hard as it is to believe it's the last day of hurricane season. And scars *still* remain from Georges.

I've made some calls, dug around a bit and I've found some statistics of note for you that you might be interested in, or perhaps not: Hurricane Georges was the deadliest hurricane within the entire Atlantic basin this season. Its 17-day journey resulted in seven landfalls (from the northeastern Caribbean to the coast of Mississippi) and 602 fatalities.

Most of the reported tornado activity associated with Georges occurred in Florida and Alabama with a total of 28 tornadoes.

In Puerto Rico, there was considerable damage to homes throughout the island. A total of 72,605 homes were damaged, of which 28,005 are estimated to have been completely destroyed. During the hurricane, over 26,000 people were in shelters. In the Dominican Republic upwards of 185,000 were left homeless by Georges and 100,000 remained in shelters through mid-October as electricity and water service remained out in most of the country. Across Haiti, government officials stated that 167,332 had been left homeless by the hurricane.

The agricultural industry in Puerto Rico was hit hard by Georges with estimates of 95% of the plantain and banana crop destroyed along with 75% of the coffee crop.

Despite Georges' weakened state when it moved across Cuba, it had a substantial impact. A total of 60,475 homes were damaged of which 3,481 were completely destroyed.

The damage to dwellings in the United States was not as extensive as that experienced across the Caribbean. In the Florida Keys 1536 homes (including ours) were damaged of which 173 were completely destroyed.

In the first 60 days or so after Georges made its final landfall in Mississippi, the American Red Cross spent $104 million on relief services in the United States Virgin Islands,

Puerto Rico, Alabama, Louisiana, Mississippi, the Florida Keys and the Florida Panhandle. This made it the most expensive disaster aid effort in the organization's 117-year history -- until Katrina.

* * *

Business is quiet at the guest house again, so Popcorn Joe has invited us out on his boat. We're thrilled, partly on account we haven't been out on a boat yet in Key West -- a travesty when you live on an island -- and partly because we didn't know Joe owned a boat.

Years back, and before Gabrielle and I married, I crewed on yachts down in Antibes, so I am quite the seafaring sod, I mean, sort, and I know just enough about powerboats and sailboats to get myself in real trouble if ever left alone at the helm -- or really anywhere onboard for that matter. The galley, for instance.

Being the generous soul he is, Joe said he would pay for the gas if we would provide sandwiches, crisps and beer. The trade seemed more than fair as these luxury yachts are thirsty beasts when it comes down to it.

We loaded Joe's pickup with enough Bud, Blue Corn Tortillas Red-Hot Blues (only available from the Waterfront Market on William Street) and sandwiches to gorge all the graduates of the Royal Naval College in Dartmouth for a week and headed off through Old Town and up North Roosevelt Boulevard. Eventually we turned down a potholed, narrow road by Banana Bay and pulled up in front of a derelict 12-foot skiff. Well, weren't we the lucky ones, Joe's yacht must be so grand it was too broad a beam and drew too much whatever yachts draw to be berthed in this modest marina!

'Probably anchored off Christmas Tree Island with all the million-dollar beauties,' I whispered to my wife.

Gabrielle and I jumped onboard, loaded the provisions and then I cast off the bowline and then the stern, and as the little dinghy slowly drifted away, we watched Joe madly waving his arms at us from the dock.

'The boat hook, shit-for-brains!' Joe yelled. 'Pull her back in with the fucking boat hook!'

'Aye, aye, skipper!' I yelled back, and then nearly harpooned Joe in the leg.

Joe threw himself onboard, commandeered the vessel and soon we were chugging happily along, parallel to Garrison Bight, following colourful buoys that would lead us in the direction of Christmas Tree Island.

The ineffectual motor on Joe's ramshackle launch juddered and sputtered as motors do when they would really rather be doing anything other than propelling a boat forward and we struggled against the tide, which was either ebbing or flooding, on our approach to the anchorage in the lee of Christmas Tree Island. And I'll tell you, there were some impressive yachts out here and Gabrielle and I wondered which one of these symbols of greed was to be our ride for the day. We cleaved the sparkling translucent waters and saw sexy Italian yachts and sleek schooners and even a floating palace with a helicopter squatting on its fantail afterdeck.

We carried on and slalomed through moored yacht after moored yacht and saw a naked lass on a powerboat, a guy named Duffy (originally from Poole) smoking a joint on a sailboat, and what appeared to be two bronzed Greek Gods rubbing baby oil all over each other on an inboard/outboard -- and that was the boat. And then just when we were almost out the other side of the anchorage, and running out of possible dream boats, we saw it before us, a pristine-white seventy-footer with a sprawling flying bridge and soaring tuna tower.

Deftly, Joe cut the motor and let his funky skiff glide silently up to the waiting yacht -- and then we rammed her broadside.

'Fucking motor's died!' Joe yelled. 'Hope the owner's not aboard.'

'This isn't your yacht?'

'What do I look like, a friggin' millionaire? I sell popcorn for chrissakes. You're sittin' on the only boat I own and right now we're on our way to Havana!'

Joe cajoled the rusty little outboard motor and tried to will it back to life, but it was having none of it. The current carried us slowly past Christmas Tree Island, and as we began applying suntan lotion for the silent voyage, we wondered if perhaps we should have brought our passports.

Eventually, Joe restored life to the outboard by adjusting the wiring, spritzing the spark plugs with WD-40 and, more importantly, giving it a swift kick with his Nike.

'Nothing like a little drama in life!' Joe proclaimed, and then pointed the bow of the boat between Christmas Tree Island and Sunset Key, and we slowly putt, putt, putted away.

Just on the other side of Christmas Tree Island the water became so shallow our little boat was just barely skimming over the patches of white sand and grassy expanses.

'These are the flats,' Joe said, 'and it goes on like this for as far as you can see.'

It may have been the first week of December now, but it was still hot and humid and we were all looking forward to a refreshing dip in the clear, glassy waters. About seven miles out we dropped anchor (actually we dropped old coffee can filled with cement) by a large patch of sand, and into the water we all jumped. The sea was only a couple of feet deep here, and we could sit on the bottom and still have our heads above the surface. The water temperature was 24 degrees and we stayed submerged, drinking beer and wallowing in the shallows.

Eventually, it was lunch time, but that was not the reason we climbed back onboard. The shark was the reason. We scrambled, laughing, but then stopped for that's when we realised the only thing separating us from this glowing example of evolution (and disfiguring scars) was about one inch of rotting plank.

'Let's get the fuck outta here!' Joe yelled.

Escape did seem prudent behaviour, so you can imagine how disconcerting it was when Joe couldn't get the outboard motor to start.

Or how we felt after an hour and the damn Evinrude still wouldn't turn over.

Or when the tide started going out.

'We have to get the boat to deeper water or we'll be stuck till the next high tide,' Joe said.

This was not exactly what we wanted to hear. Hadn't the only deep water on the trip been about an hour back?

'There's a channel over to the south. It's how the bigger boats get out to the Marquesas. If we can get her over there, I can call my friend B.O. on the mobile and he'll have to come out and pick us up. He won't be happy though.'

'Sounds good,' I said, 'but how are we going to get over to the channel?'

'We push.'

'Who pushes?' I asked, giving Gabrielle a look.

'We all push.'

'But what about Mr Jaws?'

'Let's hope we're not on the menu,' Joe joked.

And Gabrielle and I both laughed as people do when they find nothing at all humorous about a decidedly shit-you-pants' situation.

It took us a good hour, no, it was a bad hour, a god-awful hour, to push and drag the boat over the sand bits and the wide fields of shark-infested grass towards a distant island and we soon saw the edge of the channel.

'Okay, let's get back in the boat and I'll call B.O.'

We all jumped back in, glad to be out of harm's teethy way and Joe dialled his friend B.O. Then redialled. Then again. Then turned towards us with: 'Battery's low.'

Joe tried again. And again. And finally made it through: 'B.O.? Hey, it's Joe...' Then lost the signal.

Gabrielle and I looked about. If this narrow channel in front of us did indeed lead to the fishing-rich Marquesas perhaps another boat would come by.

Joe dialled yet again. Nothing. 'I'm going to try someone else.'

Joe dialled a different number and immediately was in.

'Collette? It's Joe. I'm out in the flats by Woman Key and the motor's died. Can you go ask B.O. to come out and pick us up? We're right on the edge of the channel.'

Joe listened for a moment, then repeated the instructions all over again. And then again. It was as if he were speaking to a child.

'Okay, thanks.'

Joe snapped his mobile closed: 'Hope that works. Collette is from the hinterlands of Quebec and English is an adventure for her.'

A nerve-wracking hour passed and then I spotted the shark again. 'He's back!'

'Don't think he ever really left,' Joe said.

'Gabrielle and I were, ah, digesting what Joe had just said when Joe shouted: 'Look!'

We scanned the surface of the water for the dorsal fin, expecting to see the toothy torpedo now rocketing our way.

'Not down there! Out there!' Joe yelled.

In the distance, a speck was streaking towards us. As the craft jounced closer and closer, we saw that is was our dream yacht: sleek, long, powerful and with an expansive flying bridge and impressive tuna tower.

'It's B.O.!' Joe yelled.

And within minutes, a very pissed off B.O. had Joe's disabled skiff in tow and Gabrielle and I were sitting up in the flying bridge, watching dolphins dart in front of the bow wake and laughing as B.O. good-naturedly chewed Joe a new arsehole.

Once again life was good.

And when Joe dropped us off at Villa Alberto it was a great feeling to be back home, safe and sound -- until we spotted a black Mercedes sitting in our driveway.

Gabrielle and I watched as estate-agent Bob emerged from the Merc, then a young, rich couple who appeared to be the type that would eat their young and then -- much to our horror -- Mr Tosser.

CHAPTER 19

'These people are interested in buying the cottage,' estate-wank Bob hissed. 'Is the place clean?'

'Where's the 24-hour notice, Bob?'

Bob motioned with his head towards Mr Tosser. 'Out of my hands.'

I instructed the interlopers to meet us at the front door and then Gabrielle and I dashed around the back and opened up. Inside, I quickly moved Mr Leroy's cat box out into plain view (placing on display the Cumberland sausages that Mr Leroy had taken great pride in burying), while Gabrielle took the laundry basket and scattered soiled unmentionables around the bedroom. Since we had been 'lost at sea' for the entire day, and had left only one window open, it was a furnace in the cottage, so I shut the lone window and then switched off the circuit breaker that governed the A/C.

Then I went to the front door and let the vermin in.

'Could you all be so kind and remove your shoes?'

Estate kiss-ass Bob removed his Wingtips, the wannabe snowbirds glared at us, but finally removed their northern shoes, and then, are you ready? Mr Tosser just trudged on in.

I repeated the request to remove his shoes, and do you know what our scum, slum-landlord said?

'My shoes are clean enough.'

Working the grid like a forensic team, this pack of hyenas swept through every room, peeped in every closet, opened and closed all the doors, tried the A/C (ha!), ran the shower, flushed the toilet, tried the A/C again (double ha!), tested every tap and flipped on all the lights.

Then the rich, wannabe snowbirds turned to Mr Tosser and gushed: 'If you get the A/C fixed, we'll take it!'

Gabrielle and I just stood there, stunned, as estate-commission Bob and Mr and Mrs Snotbird walked to the front door and put on their shoes. Then we metamorphosed from stunned to horrified as Mr Tosser stepped out the back door, lit up a cigar, walked across our wooden deck and climbed up into our hammock.

Christmas was less than three weeks away.

* * *

After everyone had gone, our neighbour, Snake, paid us a visit. He had seen and heard the entire miscarriage of justice.

'If your cottage sells, then mine will be the next to go -- wanna smoke a joint?'

'Thanks, but no thanks. I could kill a beer though.'

So Snake, Gabrielle and I hustled over to the Bull and we sat upstairs on the balcony overlooking heaving Duval.

It was a meeting of the War Cabinet.

Snake had been born and raised in Key West and more than once in his 50-odd years had been the victim of gentrification.

'I was born in Bahama Village in the house my father had been born in and I should still be living in that house, but goddammit,' Snake slammed his fist on the table, 'rich crackers from up north started buying up homes, the property values went sky-high and we couldn't even afford to pay the property taxes any longer.'

I ordered a margarita (heavy on the salt) for Gabrielle, a Cuba Libre (really heavy on the rum) for Snake and a pint of lager (please fill it to the bleeding top) for myself. Our drinks arrived and we just sat there in thought for a few minutes trying our best to enjoy the warm December evening.

Snake carried on: 'To stem the rising tide of gentrification in Bahama Village, the Bahama Conch Community Land Trust was created. This is a nonprofit trust and it buys up as much property as it can to take it off the real estate market. The trust buys only the land and allows the residents to maintain ownership of their homes. A good thing, and they will let you stay in your home in perpetuity.'

Snake sucked long and hard on his drink.

'Unfortunately for me, I was driven out before the trust was formed. So I rent from a piss-poor landlord who moved here not that long ago and now thinks he owns the island.'

Snake was a man of many stories, so after another pull at his coke and rum, he told us about fishing down at Mallory as a boy and sneaking into the navy base to go swimming and what back-then backwater Key West was like before the crush of tourism, the epidemic of greed and the rape of paradise.

'It's not unlike the California Gold Rush here now. It's a feeding frenzy and it's created backstabbing monsters.'

Snake was fighting a losing battle with his temper, and knew it, so he leaned over and whispered: 'Gonna go to the can and smoke a doobie. I'll order another round of drinks on the flip-flop.'

The second round of drinks arrived, followed by a greatly mellowed Snake and a waft of reefer. Snake took his Cuba Libre, held it up to the light of Duval Street below, swirled it around, then turned towards us with a conspiratorial look on his face.

'Do some of my best thinking on the shitter. Here's the straight skinny on what's coming down: That northern couple will be back tomorrow. They'll come by unannounced. Say that they just happen to be in the neighbourhood and can they have another peek at their future home. You have beautiful hardwood floors in there. Being from the frozen north, the bitch will probably measure for carpeting.'

I don't know if it was the joint or the rum or the impending thrill of the kill that appealed to a certain dark side of his character, but Snake's eyes suddenly twinkled with a devious fire.

'We're going to be ready for them this time. And here's what we're gonna do...'

Snake proceeded to explain his game plan to us and when Gabrielle and I were finally able to get our wide-open mouths slammed shut again, we were 100-per-cent certain that after tomorrow the wannabe snowbirds would never, ever, set foot in our home again.

There was a good little Cuban café down on Greene Street, so we rose early the next morning and went for Cuban coffee and Cuban bread. We wanted to enjoy the tranquillity of the early hours and fortify ourselves before the carnage began.

We sat outside under a sprawling palm tree and sipped *buccis* (Cuban coffee that could easily lift the Space Shuttle off the launching pad) and gnawed on *tostadas*. The temperature was already 20 degrees and the wind was out of the south. And there wasn't another soul around. It was peaceful and lazy and smacked of bygone days. Perhaps this is what Key West was like when Snake was growing up on the island.

We ordered another *bucci* each. Now owl-eyed, I studied my watch. Not even eight o'clock yet and already wired. A feral-esque cat approached cautiously and I didn't know if it was going to rub up against my leg, or savage me. The cat froze, eyed me, then became seemingly bored as cats do and went over into a patch of sun, rolled around a bit and eventually settled down into a non-threatening life form.

We heard a squeaking, in-need-of-oil sound in the distance and saw a lone bicyclist weaving his way from the seaport. As the bike came closer and closer, we realised it was been piloted by Captain Jerry. Geraldo, as we now called him, spotted us, gave a wave and came over to shoot the shit.

'And isn't this a fine December morn,' Geraldo said.

'Pull up a seat.'

'Don't mind if I do.'

You might remember from earlier chapters that Geraldo was quite a character, lived rough and had taken up a career of alcohol abuse.

'Want a *bucci*?' I asked.

'Coffee! Sacrilegious! Never touch the stuff!' Long beat. 'But you can make my day by giving me the money you would have spent on the *bucci*.'

Geraldo went on to tell us that he'd moved. He no longer lives at Don and Shirley's, or I should say 'under' Don and Shirley's. He tells us that he lived for a transitional fortnight in the clothing drop container located in the strip-mall car park out on North Roosevelt Boulevard.

'You lived where?'

'Y'know, one of those containers where people donate clothes and shoes.'

After it fell dark, and no one could spot him, Geraldo would simply climb up into the container and sleep on top of the donated clothes.

'What if you needed the toilet?'

'That was a problem,' Geraldo admitted. 'That's why I've relocated to some rich folk's sprawling Victorian.'

'And they don't mind you staying there?'

'They don't know that I've taken up residence. I sleep on five-star porches now. I've opted for comfort and opulence in my old age.'

I asked Geraldo if he'd ever been caught by any of the owners.

'On occasion. The upper-crust go ballistic when they catch me sleeping on the couch on their front porch.'

'And what do you do?'

'Nothing.'

'Why?'

'I have no case. Technically, I'm trespassing.'

Geraldo shifted in his chair and let the warm sun catch his face. 'But if they get their dander up and go after me, I come back later that night when alcohol knows no fear and I have a nice long pee in the swimming pool.'

'And if they don't have a pool?'

'I pee on the radiator of their car.'

'Effective,' Gabrielle said.

We told Geraldo about the problems we were having with our landlord, and Geraldo's eyes lit up.

'I've peed on his car!'

We hung out a little while longer, sawing at our Cuban bread and just enjoying the sunny morning. Then we told Geraldo about the wannabe snowbirds.

'They'll be by between nine and ten this morning,' he said.

'How do you know that?'

'They're anal-retentive. You can set your watch to people like that.'

We stayed at the café until 8:30 a.m., then we bid Geraldo adios and pedalled back home (and, yes, we gave him the money -- for his insight).

At five minutes past nine, we heard a car crunch the gravel in our driveway and looked out to see a bloody great SUV parked in our drive. Who drives an SUV around a tiny island?

'Let the carnage begin,' Gabrielle said.

We heard a loud, intrusive KNOCK, KNOCK, KNOCK -- louder than the UPS man, even -- and I opened the front door.

'Hi, we were in the neighbourhood,' the wannabes lied.

'What an unexpected surprise,' I lied.

'We just wanted to take another look. We're on our way to sign the papers.'

'C'mon in,' I said. 'Could you please remove your shoes.'

The frumpy wife threw her arms in the air exposing frightening bingo wings and gave me a cold, rich-person look: 'Must we?'

'When the place is yours, you can wear them to bed if you want.'

We watched as the couple begrudgingly removed their northern shoes and then entered our cottage.

'Does the hammock come with it?' the husband asked.

'Only the paint.'

The spawn-from-hell picked their way through the house again, touching everything that didn't belong to them and refreshing our memories of what insufferable shits they were.

The future-of-Key-West-winters cooed and oohed their way from the living room to the second bedroom/office to our bedroom and then down the hall to the bathroom. In the spirit of chivalry, I gestured for Mrs Wannabe Snowbird to enter the bathroom first and that's when the screaming began. Screaming I've only heard before in serious horror films such as *The Texas Chain Saw Massacre* or *Attack of the Killer Tomatoes*. You see, protruding out of the toilet bowl was the thick head and flicking tongue of a five-foot yellow python. The brutal shock was so great, the minger blew out the front door, arms raised, bingo wings flailing the air, followed closely by her great protector.

After Gabrielle and I finished laughing, we watched with great admiration as our neighbour, Snake, came over and extracted his pet from our commode.

'All I had to do was reach under the house and undo one joint and the snake slithered right up in there.'

Snake draped the python around his neck.

'Well, now I know where your nickname comes from,' I said.

'Oh, it's not because I like snakes,' our neighbour said, and on that he shot me a man-to-man conspiratorial wink.

And then: 'Sorry about him paying a visit during the hurricane. He probably was just lonely.'

* * *

It's the 10th of December today and estate no-commission Bob has been conspicuously absent for nearly a week. Perhaps it has something to do with Gary's Plumbing ripping up and replacing all the sewage pipes.

Just to keep our hand in it, we telephone the estate agency daily and employ fake American voices to make appointments to view Villa Alberto -- then we never show.

Our head-up-his-arse landlord has spent a fair chunk of money erecting a large eyesore sign at the end of the lane to flog the properties. Curiously, it's lasted only one night. Someone has cut it down with a chain saw.

We've paid our rent, minus the amount owed to us for the renovations, and have told Mr Tosser that if he has any problem with that to contact our nonexistent bookkeeper.

And now we're back on track to living the wonderful life we were enjoying before we were so rudely interrupted.

Cold fronts are marching through on almost a weekly basis. At night it drops into the teens and we've put on long pants for the first time in 11 months. We sleep with the windows open in Villa Alberto now and we no longer need the A/C during the day. The two-foot crawl space under our cottage that allowed our neighbour, Snake, access to our plumbing while toting a five-foot constricting machine, lets the evening breeze whistle through and our glorious hardwood floor is always cool.

Chrissy deccies are popping up like mushrooms around the island. It's strange to see twinkling coloured lights on palm trees, yachts and at the beach. And it's even stranger to see the bloke (*Yo soy de* Wyoming) giving the Jet-Ski tour wearing a Santa hat. Here, in the decidedly un-Christmas-like climate, nearly every establishment has decked the walls. Even the grills of cars and the fronts of bicycles are adorned with piney wreathes and traditional holiday bunting. And if a cold front comes through on Christmas day, we just might -- for the sake of atmosphere -- break out the woolly jumpers.

Otherwise, we're going snorkelling.

* * *

Ever since the arrival of Hurricane Georges, the island has been alive with brightly coloured little 'Disney birds'. In reality they are banana finches and they were caught up in the whirling fury as Georges moved over the island of Cuba and now they are everywhere brightening our day. These little creatures appear friendly as they fly only a few feet above the ground dipping and diving as we walk or bike around the town.

* * *

December 15th -- Business has slowed to the speed of lava down at Mallory, and our friends Tom and Sue from Brightwalton (Berkshire) are in town, so we've decided to take the night off and have the annual company Christmas Party -- even though we are affiliated with no company. It's the spirit that counts -- or is it the spirits?

There's a frightfully posh restaurant in Key West located right on the water -- sort of the tropical equivalent of The Ivy -- so we won't be going there. Instead, we've opted for B.O.'s Fish Wagon. (If you remember it was B.O. who rescued us when we almost did the *Gilligan's Island* thing with Popcorn Joe).

B.O.'s Fish Wagon is an open-air restaurant just a block from the Historic Seaport, and it's a big hit with the locals. Why is it a big hit? Well, it helps when you have funky old-wharf charm. And the tastiest food on the island. And damn friendly staff. And it doesn't hurt that it's PET FRIENDLY. Yes, you heard right. You can take your dog (and probably your snake) in there and no one will blink.

Tom and Sue own a smiley dog, two cats, four horses and chickens, so we figured they would love this place.

B.O. (whose name is Buddy Owen) gave us a wave as we entered as did his wife 'Holly'. Buddy Holly, get it? What are the chances?

We took a gander at our surroundings. The place was wall-to-wall bodies and friendly. The air mild and heady. The music loud and catchy. Sleeping at the end of the bar was B.O.'s cat. Next to the cat was a sign that read: 'Pet the Cat, $1'. Sue approached the cat, stroked it and left a pound coin in a jar. With the pound as robust as it was, this would turn into a windfall for B.O.

We sat in a corner, under a string of Christmas lights, and looked out on to William Street and we had a good laugh when a fellow with a parrot perched on his shoulder strutted in.

B.O. yelled 'Hey, Mango!' greeting the parrot and the parrot squawked back. This is where you want to spend some time when you are in Key West if you want authentic flavour. No airs and graces here. In fact, another sign says it all: 'No Shirt, No Shoes, Nooo Problem...'

A cheery, sunburnt waitress took our order, then Tom motioned to the front door as a deeply tanned bloke walked in with his black Labrador. Half the bar greeted the bloke. The other half greeted the dog.

Ever since Buddy and Holly opened the expanded version of B.O.'s Fish Wagon in 1995, they've had a friendly policy towards pets. Over any given week you can see 25 to 30 pets pay a visit. Many are accompanied by their owners. This is a place where Mr Leroy would feel at home. We will have to put him in the basket of one of our bikes and bring him along the next time.

Since the majority of pets that frequent B.O.'s Fish Wagon are dogs, each pooch is given a complimentary quarter-pound hot dog (which the Labrador is now wolfing). To quench that doggie-thirst, there's also a large community water bowl with 'No Poodles' scrawled defiantly (and as it should be) on the side.

And that says a lot about the place right there, doesn't it? It's not sexy. It's not snooty. There are no poseurs.

Only schnauzers.

A rough-looking character started knocking out obscure Christmas tunes on an upright piano (the piano sported a bumper sticker that said: SLOW DOWN! THIS AIN'T THE MAINLAND). Our dinners arrived and we sank our choppers into a commendably juicy Square Grouper Sandwich each, and enjoyed thoroughly the side of beans and rice and green olives and onions. And we flushed our systems with a company-Christmas Party portion of alcohol. And the music and the creatures and the food and the Christmas lights and the smells made it all exotic and very far-flung indeed. And we still couldn't believe that we were living in Key West. That we had given up everything back home. That we had stayed.

We were feeling the emotion of the moment.

I held up my beer.

Tom held up his beer.

Sue and Gabrielle held up their red wine.

And we clinked plastic.

* * *

We've purchased a real Christmas tree but can't get it back home on our bikes, so the man wearing shorts at the lot has delivered it in the back of his convertible. Our Christmas tree, which appeared symmetrical and full among its friends, has in reality an open back like the gowns patients wear at hospitals.

We are about to trim the Christmas tree -- and to put everything into perspective -- it's the 18th of December and 25 degrees outside. Are you getting the picture here? Is it coming into focus? Loud and clear? We've never trimmed a Christmas tree in 25-degree weather and shorts before. It's an odd feeling. Sartorially surreal even.

Mr Leroy is in charge of quality control. Before we hang an ornament on the tree, he has to play with it. The round ones he deftly scoots across the hardwood floor Michael Owen-style. The odd shaped ones we suspend from a lower branch and he bats them as a boxer does a punching bag. Now Mr Leroy has decided to take a little break from his duties and he's collapsed in the hammock. A cat lying asleep on its back in a hammock is an inordinately adorable sight.

Believe it or not there is a Christmas store in Key West that's open all year round. And this makes perfect sense, doesn't it, an all-year-round Christmas store on a tropical island? I'm sure there must be a shop in Lillehammer that sells bikinis all year round. Or a shop in Texas longhorn country that sells vegetarian shoes.

We've set up the Christmas tree in the living room -- right next to the air conditioner. Theoretically, it is feasible we could have the Christmas tree lights and the A/C on at the same time. This is too much for our once East Sussex mind-set to handle, so we've banished the image.

Our Christmas tree stand has come with one of those little packets of orange 'polygel' you see for sale in Spain at the markets. You only have to add water and a pokey amount of polygel expands to colossal proportions.

We've strung the lights now and, get ready, positioned a once real-live starfish at the top of the tree. We purchased the starfish at a place down by Mallory Square called the Shell Warehouse. The sight of the starfish atop our tree next to the A/C is too hilarious for words (so these will have to do).

We don't have a fireplace, so Gabrielle has hung three stockings on the air conditioner. There's a stocking for 'Gabrielle', 'Jon' and 'Mr Leroy'. We're not sure if Mr Leroy knows which stocking is his, but we think he has picked up the scent of the catnip.

Oh my God! What's that? Just outside our front window a young lass is riding a bicycle down the lane, but that's not the Oh-my-God part, the Oh-my-God part is that she's wearing a Santa hat and matching bikini.

Quelle incongruous sight!

* * *

It's now the 21st of December, the shortest day of the year, and we're having the longest night of our lives.

We have rats again.

Lots of them.

They have arrived in time for the holidays.

We can hear them at night running amok behind the walls of Villa Alberto. They sound more like a herd of buffalo. Remember *Dances With Wolves*? That sound. Only right behind your pillow.

Our dear neighbour across the street, Mrs Grace, says they have been driven in by the colder weather (these rats don't know what cold weather is!). Apparently they have been living in our palm trees. When Mrs Grace sits on her porch at night in her rocking chair, imitating a metronome, she can see them using the telephone cable on the side of our cottage as a highway.

We've been living next to the rat-world equivalent of that stretch of the M6 in Birmingham and didn't know it.

The little buggers keep odd hours. We've been wakened the past two nights now, so this morning we went down to Strunk Hardware and purchased rat poison. The lethal toxin is in fact not a toxin, rather an anticoagulant -- warfarin. The rats eat the bait and then simply bleed internally until they die. I know. I know. But I had to tell you.

Our neighbour, Snake, doesn't have a rat problem -- he has a five-foot long, yellow rat repeller. All things considered, we'd take beady-eyed Ben over the yellow rat repeller.

* * *

It's Christmas Eve. In a little over two weeks we will have been in Key West for one year. It's spooky how fast tempus fugit.

To celebrate Christmas Eve, we have invaded our local, the Bull & Whistle, and this is where we are now, sitting in one of the open front windows looking out on to teeming Duval Street. This is one of those places (like Raffles in Singapore) where if we sit here long enough, everyone we know on the face of the earth will pass by, albeit hammered. Christmas Eve and we're sitting in a bar, but it seems the right place to be. It's 8 o'clock, 20 degrees and the music is merry, merry good.

'Merry Christmas!' we hear someone shout. We look up to see none other than Shark-Man riding by on his bicycle. He's deeply tanned as always and is sporting a tank top to show off his plentiful muscles and a necklace of shark teeth. A rough bloke, but a sucker for the holiday spirit Gabrielle decides, Shark-Man is wearing antlers on his head.

It's great to see Shark-Man -- as we haven't seen him since chapter eight -- and somehow his antlered joie de vivre brings out the holiday spirit in us even more.

Flushed with goodwill toward man, I order a couple of eggnogs heavily laced with brandy. The eggnogs arrive and after a few quick sups the searing brandy begins to work its magic and we cast our minds back over the nearly 12 months that we have resided on this tropical isle at the end of the world.

We'd arrived radiantly peelie-wally but now were brown as berries. We'd found jobs, secured a place to live and owned rusty old modes of conveyance. We lived on an island closer to Havana than Miami and you could trim your Christmas tree in shorts and hang your Christmas stockings on the A/C.

And we'd adopted Mr Leroy.

Or had he adopted us?

We'd taken root in a part of the globe where the Weather Channel dictates existence and becomes a close friend. Where you learn what an Intertropical Convergence Zone is. And where uninvited guests under the guise of Mother Nature's fury come calling between the 1st of June and the 30th of November.

And we hadn't been arrested yet.

Gabrielle and I sat there in a giddy aura of happiness and watched the world go by and talked about everything under the stars. When Christmas Eve was turning to Christmas morn, we exited the Bull, stage right, and walked home, arm and arm, up Duval Street, and then we cut through the

Mobster Lobster to pick up Mr Leroy who was just finishing his shift.

At Villa Alberto, we opened up our Christmas presents (it was a catnip mouse), and then we all climbed up into our hammock, watched the stars twinkling at us from above and let the fragrance of night-blooming jasmine wash over us.

And just before we fell asleep, we heard off in the distance somewhere *Silent Night* playing -- on a steel drum.

EPILOGUE:

Gabrielle has since thrown her lawlessness directly into the face of the prevailing Westerlies and now proudly possesses a US passport. Subsequently, her photograph has been dutifully removed from all post offices in south Florida.

* * *

If you've enjoyed **KEY WEST**, check out **NAKED EUROPE: In the Hunt for the Real Europe—and Romance**, soon available as an eBook on Amazon.

For those of you lusting for grittier fayre, **DEATH BY GLASGOW**, a crime/thriller set in the means streets of Glasgow, Scotland, will be hitting the bookshelves soon.

WAIT! Yes, wait! I've decided to write a seagull, I mean, a sequel. Keep your contacts in and keep both eyes on Amazon for **KEY WEST: the Sequel...**

18113881R00128

Made in the USA
Lexington, KY
15 October 2012